THE PYRAMIDS
OF EGYPT

THE PYRAMIDS OF EGYPT

EMMANUEL BARCELÓ

© EDIMAT BOOKS Ltd. London
is an affiliate of Edimat Libros S.A.
C/ Primavera, 35 Pol. Ind. El Malvar
Arganda del Rey - 28500 (Madrid) Spain
E-mail: edimat@edimat.es

Title: *The Pyramids of Egypt*
Author: *Emmanuel Barceló*

ISBN: 84-9794-029-6
Legal Deposit: M-48227-2004

PRINTED IN SPAIN

INTRODUCTION

Can the secret of certain lost sciences, philosophy and religion be found inside the pyramids? Perhaps were these remainders of the Seven Wonders of the World, which on infinite occasions have been worthy of being described as the most sublime deeds in history, built by wise architects, all of them initiates, who managed to achieve such profound knowledge that it could be comparable to that held by extra-terrestrials or a "chosen" civilisation?

Many researchers point to the most advanced theories, letting their imaginations fly, while others limit themselves to what has been discovered by archaeology, traditional science and the writings found in Egypt. But the latter cannot fail to acknowledge that that are facing deeds that are virtually impossible to explain using academic methodology: the process of mummification in all its complexity; the structure of the pyramids; the secret placement of the passageways; the way they were constructed; the millions of artistic testimonials; the fact that iron artefacts have been found in the tombs; and so many other things...

"Astounding!"

This is the exclamation made by the conservative investigator, especially when forced to accept that he is judging a civilisation that populated the Nile Valley more than 6,000 years ago and that later dominated it throughout 21 centuries. If they focus on a single fact, such as the trepanation of a human cranium to perform brain operations, how many questions must be formulated when comparing this knowledge to that of the Middle Ages or even the Renaissance?

The Egyptians must have known about complete anaesthesia in order to perform surgical operations that today require more than six hours using the most sophisticated instruments, when anaesthesia only reached the field of medicine last century. We could also mention the scalpels and medical drills, which allowed the cranium to be opened, something that "modern" surgeons learned to do in the eighteenth century.

The slow awakening of a volcano

The world knew about the existence of ancient Egypt through books, the ruins that remained in the desert and legends. The fact that this country spent so many centuries dominated by Arabs, who had fruitlessly tried to wrest the treasures from the pyramids, left these physically buried in the desert sands. At the same time, they had suffered so much significant damage, losing their polished marble outer coverings and being "attacked" by canons and small firearms that they appeared like the ruins of feudal castles that have been left to the mercy of the elements.

But the conquest of Egypt by Napoleon's army brought with it such a need to "explore the stones" that a human flood reached the Nile Valley with something more than a tourist's curiosity. If indeed it is unfortunate that it took a war to awaken the world's interest in this ancient civilisation, we must bear in mind that it led to great artists' illustrating books so rich in fascinating descriptions and drawings that it unleashed what we could call "Egypt-mania".

But with his deciphering of the Egyptian hieroglyphics found on the Rosetta Stone, Champollion managed to eliminate the rubble covering the mouth of an enormous volcano. As the papyrus, tablets and rocks extracted from the pyramids and the temples were being read, as were the sphinxes, obelisks and other buildings and ruins, Egyptian civilisation began to blossom.

The ever-more fascinating volcano that is Egypt began to erupt slowly, unleashing passions and feeding myths. Soon figures such as the Italian Captain G. B. Caviglia arrived, willing to spend his last penny to discover the mysteries of the Great Pyramid of Cheops. His contemporaries had even described him thus:

... He feels so fascinated by these sanctuaries of ancient science that he has sacrificed his family with the sole purpose of satisfying his refined tastes, because he sees the mysteries hidden in the Pyramids and the tombs as the supreme challenge...

Caviglia would come to his ruin in Egypt, just like a lover who attempts to besiege the most implacable beauty. Since this did not lead him to abandon his obsession, he stayed there to help other researchers and did not mind on occasion sacking the entrails of his adored Pyramids. He even let gunpowder be used in the subterranean galleries, close to the tombs where the pharaohs and princesses rested in their millennial dreams. But we shall leave the denouement of this astounding story for another occasion.

Great knowledge for "initiates"

In the middle of the century a small group of investigators, most of them English, began to measure the pyramids. They did so with the greatest precision, comparing their data with what had been written to date. In this way, much more disturbing elements were added to an already dazzling, magical story: confirmation that the Egyptian architects could make mathematical and geometrical calculations that had "always" been attributed to certain Greek sages, and at the same time the discovery that the pyramids had not been constructed haphazardly. All of them are placed on an exact geodesic point; their orientation was highly precise and they could in fact be used as gigantic astronomical observatories, and at the same time for other more complex functions. Was it possible to consider them immense libraries of the most prodigious knowledge from the ancient world?

It is no coincidence that the foundations of the most colossal buildings ever constructed by human beings, larger than the cathedrals, were oriented precisely toward the north; nor that in their structure the value of *pi* (the constant used to multiply the diameter of a circle to obtain its circumference) was used to a degree of accuracy of four decimal points; nor that in their main chambers triangles were used with the equation $a^2 + b^2 = C^2$, which later became known around the world as the Pythagorean theorem, and which Plato, in his work Timaeus, considered the main building block of the cosmos.

Nor is it possible to doubt that the angles used to measure the triangles, those that form the façades of the pyramids, show that their designers knew trigonometry, when it had always been believed that in Egypt they had never gone beyond mere addition.

We have here a small part of the great discoveries made by the wise Egyptians, many of which we will explain in our book. These wise men were initiates, superior beings, almost gods, who had created their own hermetic language to communicate among themselves, as have the majority of the best-known religious sects.

A religion that attempted to treat gods "as equals"

The Egyptian pharaohs were considered gods, while their priests taught "tricks" to "fool" the tribunal of divinities that judged the dead. In their prayers they treated the gods "as equals"; thus they threatened them with ceasing to make offerings or with taking away those that had been left at the altars.

With its rich mythology, in which some of their great gods such as Osiris and Horus had so much in common with the Christian Virgin and Jesus, they considered many animals to be sacred. When one of these died, its owners would shave their eyebrows if it was a cat, or their heads and the rest of the body if it was a dog. Later they would embalm them and bury them in a hidden place. The proof of this rite was found in a gigantic underground necropolis, from which since the beginning of 1952 more than four million small sarcophagi have been extracted.

Let us return to the terrain of the sciences

The most recent studies have demonstrated that in Egypt, *pi* began to be used in the year 1700 BC, at least ten centuries after the construction of the first pyramid. The Pythagorean theorem only dates from the year 500 BC, and the development of trigonometry is attributed to Hipparchus in the second century BC Peter Tompkins wrote this in his book, "Secrets of the Great Pyramid":

Throughout almost a thousand years, there has been the idea that a group of men have come to work to shed light on the true purpose of the pyramids. Through their own means, each of them has discovered a valid facet. Just as with Stonehenge and other megalithic calendars, it has been shown that the Pyramid of Cheops constitutes an almanac, through which it is possible to measure the length of a year, even up to the minuscule fraction of 0.2422 for one day, which is the degree of precision found in a modern-day telescope. It has been demonstrated that it acted as a theodolite, a highly simple, highly precise measuring instrument which is physically indestructible. Nowadays it continues to act as a compass gauged with such accuracy that modern compasses have to be adjusted to it, not it to them.

It has also been firmly established that the Great Pyramid is a geodesic marker that is meticulously placed; that is, it is a fixed landmark from which the geography of the ancient world was brilliantly constructed. It was also used as a celestial observatory from which maps and tables of the stellar hemisphere could be traced with great accuracy. At the same time, its façades and angles constitute the means to create an extraordinarily detailed geographic projection of the southern hemisphere. It is, in fact, a scale model of the hemisphere in which the geographical degrees of latitude and longitude can be observed with exactness.

Here we have testimony that admits no doubts as to the exceptional importance of the pyramids, since what Tompkins says about the Great Pyramid can be applied to the others as well.

But we are concerned with enigmas

We believe that with many of the elements mentioned above, we have already put forth enough enigmas without having to formulate one categorically; nevertheless, we shall do so in a few cases:

"How could the Egyptian initiates have obtained so much knowledge, the majority of which was superior or equal to ours, at a time in which they were almost closer to prehistoric man than to the twentieth century?"

"What means did they have at their disposal for moving millions of blocks of granite, some of which weighed seventy tonnes, from the quarries to the Nile valley?"

"How did they cut and assemble these blocks, when it has been proven that their fit is so precise that not even a human hair could be inserted between them?"

"Should we assume that the ancient Egyptians were helped by beings that 'came from outer space', by a highly evolved civilisation in flight from the great cataclysms that had taken place in Asia, or by the survivors of Atlantis?"

"Is it possible that in the interior galleries of the Great Pyramid the great prophecies telling about the beginning of the existence of human beings on Earth until their end in the cosmos are hidden?"

"Should we believe that the roots of the Judeo-Christian religions were born in Egypt?"

"Might the Great Pyramid, solely due to its shape and orientation, conserve food, improve the functioning of many elements, emit unknown energies and even solve highly complex problems?"

Chapter I

PAPYRUS AND STONES

Twenty-five centuries of prodigies

If Egyptian civilisation is evaluated through the prism of archaeology, what remains is a succession of pyramids, mummies, figures of pharaohs, queens and important personages and many other things – nothing more than objects, from the most monumental to those of infinitesimal size. All in the past.

Yet, as we delve deeper into the impressive ruins, as we analyse the shock caused by the bandaged cadavers, as we admire the beauty of the statues and coffins of the great monarchs and their gods, and as we study the impressive range of their mythology, one does not have to be highly sensitive to realize that we are facing something exceptional. It was an indelible landmark in the history of humankind and it attracts our curiosity, it fascinates us, as we see it surrounded by so many mysteries and enigmas.

Forty centuries look down upon us from the heights of these pyramids, exclaimed Napoleon Bonaparte. The most curious thing is that the French emperor, who was one of the most famous figures in the modern era and indeed from all time, was only seeing a minuscule part of so many marvels, due to the fact that almost all the pyramids were physically buried under the sand and no one yet knew what was hidden inside them.

Ancient Egyptian civilisation lasted almost 25 centuries, pretty much the most fabulous civilisation ever known on our planet. It lasted some 35 generations, if a generation is counted every 75 years. During this time great battles were fought, with sensational victories and shameful defeats; passionate loves were awoken and incest was even exalted; and the greatest funerary monuments were constructed.

All of this happened on the banks of the Nile, the mightiest in the world and that which has awoken the greatest passions, with its three months per year of flooding that left lands as fertile as those found in a paradise. There an empire, or various empires, were born, flourished and died, leaving testimony as astounding as it is enigmatic.

Father Nile, who so often acted as a mother

The Nile River has been there since the beginning of time as a witness to the rise of so many prodigies, and later to a period of downfall, until arriving at modern-day Egypt. Thanks to the Greek historians such as Herodotus, we know that the inhabitants of the banks of this immense waterway built dykes for wars but never to water their crops, perhaps because they were so sure that each year the gift from the gods would arrive with the floods, those yearned for surges that filled the lands with lime and natural fertiliser while they also moistened the depths of the lands just like a powerful stud with a healthy, vigorous female.

The Nile originates in the depths of Black Africa – its sources were discovered at the end of the last century; it crosses Sudan near Khartoum, its capital, and it acquires all its grandeur at the joining of its two main branches, the White Nile and the Blue Nile. In its lengthy course, it forms waterfalls in the deserts of Nubia and reaches Egypt, which treated it as if it were a generous father who on occasion acted as a mother. (Here we have started to speak in the past since all this changed with the construction of the giant Aswan Dam between 1957 and 1963).

In Egypt, the sand seems to disappear on the banks of this already might river, and a calcareous soil appears which soon becomes filled with verdure and vegetation. Yet in narrow areas it began to gradually broaden, something that is quite normal in any fluvial landscape, especially given the annual floods.

These floods became a blessing for a country where it never rained because they allowed the farmers to attain up to two harvests per year. The Nile became Egypt's father from June to October; then, by November it had recovered its normal flow. As is logical, the country did not take advantage of this entire period of bonanza since in the south the floods arrived in June and disappeared three months later, something that did not happen in Cairo, where the flow went back to normal during the month of November.

The Nile also acted as a type of border for ancient Egypt since it isolated it from neighbouring countries. Since it supported such agricultural richness, while in the desert gold, silver and turquoise mines could be found, it is not surprising that some of the pharaohs did not seek to limit their expenditures when building pyramids, which required more than twenty years of labour and almost half a million architects, craftsmen, operators and soldiers as well as the families of all of these.

The great "Rome"

The "Rome" (the "men"), as the ancient Egyptians called them, lived in the Nile Valley. The first history of Egypt comes down to us from Manethon, a scribe and priest who finished his work during the time of the Ptolemies, from the end of the fourth century until the middle of the second century BC He made a list of all the kings from his country in 31 dynasties, each one individualised according to different criteria: coming from the same family, from the same city, and others that were more complex.

Despite the fact that this work contains various errors, it is crucial if one wishes to make a broad sketch of the land of the pharaohs. The great "Rome" lived in times of splendour, downfall, confusion and anarchy. Once the Pre-dynastic period was over, before the time recorded in history, three imperial cycles were begun, as were the same number of kingdoms or empires, two stages of decline and two more intense "intermediate periods".

In this way, the history of the 31 dynasties can be divided in the following way: The Dynastic Period, the first period after the country was unified; the Old Empire, followed by a violent period known as the First Intermediate Period which then led to the Middle Empire. Egypt was almost destroyed due to fratricidal wars which various foreign invaders joined, but then it was recovered in the New Empire, which began just after the end of the Second Intermediate Period.

After the New Empire there was a Third Intermediate Period, and then the Late Empire, which hosted a renaissance known as the "Saite Era" after the name of the capital of the empire. Regarding the dynasties, the Old Empire attained its greatest splendour under the reign of the fourth, fifth, and sixth dynasties; the Middle Empire during the eleventh and twelfth dynasties; and the New Empire during the eighteenth, nineteenth and twentieth dynasties.

How Egypt came into existence

All the great ancient civilisations began to exist at the moment in which they learned how to write down their reality. It is calculated that writing began in Egypt some 6,000 years ago. The first system consisted of figurative hieroglyphics, in which the object represented was simply drawn. This primitive system gradually began to use ideograms and phonograms, which brought with them abstractions and sounds. Twenty-four hieroglyphics were used to represent the same number of consonant sounds. Later, another 24 were incorporated to represent polysyllabic sounds. Nevertheless, an alphabetical writing system never managed to be developed.

Teaching this type of writing proved to be so complex that it took many years, turning scribes into the most highly valued artisans in the palaces and temples.

This writing system was used almost until the late years of Egyptian domination, always using stones, walls and statues as the means on which to write what they wished to communicate. However, with the invention of papyrus, the scribes simplified the hieroglyphics, even resorting to hieratic or priestly writing, which was also used on tablets.

Another type of writing, the demotic or popular, could be found on papyrus dating from Egyptian civilisation's process of agony in around 700 BC

Earliest myths and legends

The texts from ancient Egypt that can be considered strictly literary have generally reached us on this fragile material made from the pulp of the papyrus plant pressed into sheets. Their ideographic writing system was indecipherable until the beginning of the nineteenth century. Among the most ancient works we know about are the books called the "Wisdom", which were compilations of precepts and moral maxims, such as the one attributed to Prime Minister Imhotep (2800 BC), which is lost today, and the still-conserved one by Ptahhotep, who must have lived around the year 2400 BC "Dialogue of the Desperate Man" comes from 2300 BC and describes a man who is fed up with existence and injustice and desires death, but his instinct impels him to grasp onto the idea that in spite of everything, the most important thing is to live and to enjoy all of life's pleasures.

At the beginning of the second millennium, with the arrival of the twelfth pharaonic dynasty, a period of literary splendour began. The "Hymn of the Nile" belongs to this period, a jubilant song to all of nature in appreciation of the benevolent rising of the river; the "Satire of the Crafts", which attempts to separate students from the manual crafts in order to encourage them to cultivate the letters which will enable them to become scribes; and the novella "Sinuhe, The Egyptian", a name that became so popular throughout the world during the 1960s thanks to the work by the contemporary author, Mika Waltari.

This tale recounts the flight of the hero, kin to a murdered pharaoh, in fear that he might be found guilty of having participated in the plot. Sinuhe reaches Asia, and when he is about to die of thirst, he is recognised by a Bedouin chief who gives Sinuhe his daughter's hand in marriage. He manages to become a highly prestigious tribal chief among the Syrians, but in his dotage he feels nostalgic for Egypt and returns to his homeland, where Sesotris I receives him benevolently.

After the crisis of the seventeenth century BC was overcome, and the subsequent invasion by the Hyksos, Egyptian literature shows a certain satirical tone, especially in the harpist's chant recorded in a real tomb. With the New Empire, profane and religious poetry arrive, such as the effusive hymns composed by Amenophis IV, the reforming pharaoh, for the only god, Aten. The famous "Book of the Dead" is worth special mention, and we will save its description for a later time.

From the twelfth century BC come the tales "The Two Brothers" and "Ani's Wisdom", which is advice from a father to his son, a work which was concluded during the New Empire. At that time Egyptian literature experienced a clear downfall. In the eighth century BC we could cite "Wisdom of Amenemope" as one of the last important samples of writers from the country of the pharaohs.

The Rosetta Stone

When Napoleon Bonaparte decided to conquer Egypt in 1798, he was so astonished by the pyramids that he ordered studies to be made on the culture of this country. Among the many objects his army took as booty can be found a stele made of black basalt which had been located near the city of Rosetta.

A decree by the pharaoh Ptolemy V, dated 196 BC, had been written on this stone in three languages (Greek, demotic and hieroglyphics). From the start it was clear that this was a very important find, since various copies of it were made before it was appropriated by an English captain, who took it to London, where it was kept in the British Museum.

The Rosetta Stone sparked the interest of linguists, especially the young Frenchman, Jean-François Champollion, a genius for learning oriental languages whose knowledge included the majority of those spoken in the countries around Egypt. It took him 14 years of research until he was able to decipher the first hieroglyphics.

In this way, the Rosetta Stone and Champollion opened the mind of the world to the wonders and sciences of ancient Egypt, whereas the only interest prior to that time had been visual or rapine.

The initiates wanted it that way

Initiates into all sects and religions are instructed so that, from the moment in which they cease to be neophytes or apprentices, they become aware that the rules and teachings they will receive must be protected from common people and outsiders. For this reason, a secret language, ritualised gestures or a series of internal communications are used, giving shape to an exclusive universe only for the privileged.

The Pyramids were constructed as a means of universal, encyclopaedic and cosmic communication, only meant to be understood by initiates. So if these initiates had their own language, much more complex and difficult to interpret than these hieroglyphics engraved in the rocks or drawn on the tablets, why would they bother to create a more popular language?

It was enough for the initiates to satisfy their own egos, since they were considered superior beings, gods. Within the theories put forth until now to explain certain enigmas, if the initiates had been instructed by beings who had come from outer space, they could have provided ordinary people with some of this knowledge, while reserving the most important knowledge for themselves.

Who were these initiates?

Although we will speak about them in plenty of detail later on, it is worth clarifying the fact that these beings could have been magician-priests or pharaohs, just like the architects who built the pyramids or the scribes who left us the hiero-glyphics on tablets, papyrus and subterranean walls. They were all superior beings.

Almost gods. They received their knowledge from Asian civilisations that escaped from large-scale cataclysms to find refuge on the fertile banks of the Nile, from men who came from outer space, or perhaps they simply acquired this knowledge through their own means. Nevertheless, their wisdom was so broad, they brought together so much magic and mystery, that they did not dare communicate it to inferior beings, perhaps for fear that it would drive them crazy. This is why they decided to convert the pyramids into great libraries of the occult, into immense astronomical observatories, into solar timepieces, into a compendium of the prophecies of what was going to occur throughout more than 80 centuries, and into many other things.

Just as the great religions and secret sects tend to do, the Egyptian sages used hermetic arts, or secrecy, to communicate among themselves and so that their knowledge could be discovered by future generations. Yet they refused to make access to this knowledge too easy, thus they made use of geometry and mathematics to erect a barrier against savagery and ignorance. This strength and obstinacy would have been worthless had it not been accompanied by patience and open-mindedness in order to vanquish the great seals that protected a millennial science.

These seals were gradually opened, step by step, by different Egyptologists or pyramid experts, many of whom will be cited in our book. They all realized immediately that they were facing an enterprise by Titans, a work made by exceptional beings. This is why investigating them was so fascinating that on many occasions it drove people mad or even to their death. All because they wanted to follow the trail of the great initiates from the Egypt of the pyramids.

18

Chapter II

EGYPT, WHERE THE FABULOUS WAS EVERYDAY

It happened more than 4000 years ago

The mythical Egypt did not know the meaning of the word "impossible". Governed by pharaohs who were believed to be gods, each enterprise they carried out culminated in success, even if in achieving this they had to mobilise the entire nation and use economic resources that would seem inconceivable today.

Within the limits of our modern-day society, it seems even harder to believe that more than forty centuries, ago works as fabulous as the pyramids could have been made, when these were just meant to be the greatest tombs ever known by humanity... Perhaps they were trying to hide inside them a body of knowledge, astral references and other erudition that were only within the reach of the sages or the initiates?

If we bear in mind that the current pyramids are just the remains of the primitive ones, given the spoils they have suffered, we can imagine that the most fabulous architectural works carried out by human beings must have been extraordinarily beautiful. They were originally covered by a layer of shiny slabs which converted them into a type of large lighthouses which were torn up in order to construct vulgar buildings on the banks of the Nile.

As tombs, the pyramids were provided with secret chambers which could be accessed through labyrinths that could only be followed by the architects who designed them. In this way they ensured the eternal rest of the pharaohs and their families, as well as their trusted associates. This objective was attained for many aeons until the Muslims broke through the first barriers. Nevertheless, it was not until the nineteenth century that the systematic and unstoppable process of desecrating the great mysteries was begun.

The setting of the pyramids

Some 100 miles from the current city of Cairo there is a rocky landscape which appears just at the edge of a terrain covered with tamarind, acacia and eucalyptus trees. On a surface area that is almost 21 square feet it is possible to see the entire group of approximately 164 feet-high palm trees of the Nile Valley. From this surface, named Giza by the Arabs, which has been flattened through human effort, one can also reach the Great Pyramid of Cheops. Toward the west extend the broad sands of the Libyan desert.

The base of this pyramid covers almost 10 acres, which equals some eight large city blocks. Within this broad esplanade, which is smooth up to one inch, and under the cloudless blue Egyptian skies, were erected something more than two and a half million blocks of limestone and granite (each one weighing between two and seventy tonnes), in 201 stepped rows, covering the approximate height of a modern-day, 42-storey building.

If we judge this construction in terms of pure brickwork, we must point out that when it was built, more stone was used than in all the cathedrals, churches and chapels that have been built in some European countries since the birth of Jesus Christ, such as in England, Ireland or Denmark. Many of today's architects still cannot comprehend how they could resolve so many problems with such primitive means, reaching the utter precision of the overall complex.

When the Great Pyramid was finished, with its entire exterior covered with polished limestone, it must have been overwhelming for the eyes. It was surely not built of marble because they knew that this would end up being eroded by the intense desert heat, the lack of humidity and time; this is why they chose to use a more resistant material.

Near the Pyramid of Cheops there are two other smaller pyramids. One is attributed to the pharaoh Khafre, who was Cheops' successor, and the other to Mencaure, who followed the Khafre. Relatively close by there are six smaller pyramids, which must have served as tombs for Cheops' wives and daughters. Continuing on the western bank of the Nile toward the south, another one hundred pyramid complexes appear, all of them in various stages of deterioration. They cover a space of almost 62 miles, but none of them is larger in size and dimensions than the Great Pyramid, and this is why this pyramid will become one of the main focuses of our book.

The pyramids were not founded on thousands of human lives

For tragedy-loving literature, it is essential to imagine that the pyramids were built on the foundations of hundreds of thousands of cadavers. How many great myths have relied on human sacrifice in order to become universal?

We will not dare to say that this fabulous construction, in which an entire nation participated almost throughout its entire existence, was built entirely without losses. Obviously there were deaths, perhaps more than in any modern-day construction project, even if they were few in number. No one can avoid unforeseen accidents, especially in that age when mechanical elements were hardly known and brute, physical force was the essential tool. The German historian, Hermann Junker, tells us the following:

It has never failed to amaze me to see that in ancient Egypt the family constituted the social base, just as friendship and treating inferiors well were considered natural. The powerful believed that it was their ineluctable obligation to help the poor and oppressed. If we examine the kings' and pharaohs' decisions, we can see that the majority of them were examples of rectitude and humanity. I have never found evidence that would lead me to believe that there was a slave trade, leaving aside the fact that slaves at that time could be compared to servants today; I have never found reference to human beings subjugated to the whip, to food being rationed, while obligating them to work from sunup to sundown, on many occasions without being concerned whether they lost their lives, knowing that it was very easy to substitute one for another. This is why Egyptian slaves, if indeed we can call them slaves, were never separated from their masters, because they knew they formed part of the family...

Nor is it logical to think that prisoners of war were used to construct the pyramids, since Egypt never took enough prisoners in their numerous battles. In reality, the millions of workers who participated in this fabulous, colossal project must have contributed their efforts voluntarily, not only because in this way they had work, perhaps at a time when the Nile was not as generous as it had been in previous years, but also because they enjoyed the enterprise.

If the perfect carving of the large stones, the exact precision of their assembly and the mathematical rigour of their architecture are examined, one can conclude that martyred workers, who were frightened of the whip that besieged them, could never have been able to create such a crowning achievement. The best proof of this can be found in the funerary temple of Menkaure, where the projecting strips that protected the edges of the stones during transport and which were taken off just before the stone was installed in its appropriate place were conserved. Seeing these strips, one can observe the mastery of the carver, who knew that the great stones had to fit together perfectly, without using anything more than a light mortar, so that not even a human hair could be inserted between the stones.

The greatest geometricians

The construction of the pyramids was carried out by architects who can be considered the greatest masters of geometry of all time. The calculations that they had to perform in order to erect the gigantic triangles, each composed of millions of stones, lead us to imagine them as sages that had access to mysterious rules of calculation. Is it possible that they did it all using simple mathematical operations? Can we believe that they only knew how to add, as some historians have claimed?

Having reached this point, should we think about cosmic or astronomical secrets, the assistance of beings who came from outer space, or other similar types of help? We shall leave the answers to these questions for further on, since for now we are more interested in pursuing the more orthodox path.

The Englishman, John Taylor, was the first to discover that when you divide the perimeter of the pyramids by twice their height, you obtain a quotient of 3.144, which was a value very close to that of *pi*, which is 3.14159+. In other words, the height of the pyramid seemed to show the same relationship as the radius of a circle to its circumference.

Since this discovery seemed to Taylor to be too extraordinary to be sheer coincidence, he ended up reaching the conclusion that the calculation of Egyptian geometry was based on an incommensurable of *pi*. Accepting this proposition meant attributing prodigious mathematical knowledge to the pyramid builders. We must bear in mind that at that time it was believed that the exact value of *pi* had been discovered by the Hindu sage Arya Bhata, but only up to the fourth decimal point. Modern calculators have provided us with up to 10,000 decimal points yet have not reached the exact value, something that Egyptian geometricians apparently knew.

This, however, is not demonstrated by the Rhind papyrus, which has been dated from 1700 BC, meaning that it is from considerably later than the construction of the pyramids. It was found among the wrappings of a mummy in 1855 by a Scottish archaeologist named Henry Alexander Rhind, and it is currently preserved in the British Museum. This papyrus has a relatively inexact value of *pi*: 3.16.

It is possible that the knowledge of the geometricians who built the pyramids was lost along with them, becoming reduced, in part, as it was taught to the future generations.

Nevertheless, Taylor made other more astounding discoveries, which we shall divulge when the time comes.

The Pyramids ended up speaking

The earliest Pyramids built can be considered "mute". The majority of them come from the powerful fourth dynasty of pharaohs. They did not begin to "speak" until the third millennium before Christ, when the minor pyramids of Unas, Teti and Merenre were erected. At that time, hieroglyphs were engraved and painted inside the burial chambers, leaving evidence of a magnificent past and present. The cultural testimony of a unique civilisation was left through these, just like in a library. The German historian, Kurt Lange described one of his first explorations in this way:

On the stone-beamed ceiling, which was made to resemble a night time sky, appeared lines of five-pointed stars, which still preserved remnants of their brilliant colour from the past. Since their founding in the year 1881, when forced entry into the pyramids was finally achieved, these texts are among the most precious documentation we have on the primitive history of the religions, since they are the most ancient holy formulas. If we consider the fact that everywhere mortuary ceremonies tend to take place in the same way throughout time, we can deduce that the oldest formulas come from King Djoser. Thus they correspond to the time in which the earliest stone constructions worthy of this name emerged, the same time as the earliest events that have been recorded in the history of human civilisation. All of this supports the idea that we are facing a much more ancient heritage, the first religious samples of Egyptian sensibility...

The texts sculpted or painted onto the stone in the form of hieroglyphics were not mere testimonies to history, since on many occasions they also showed a high literary quality. As an example we shall see what they told about the celestial journey of King Unas:

He shall no longer sleep in the tomb, so he shall prevent his bones from disintegrating. The ailments and pains that led him to death have disappeared. The king is flying heaven-

24

ward. He has undertaken this as a cloud, in a flight similar to that of the grey heron. He shall soon kiss the sky like a falcon. He shall enter into paradise just as a swarm of grasshoppers darkens the sun. He shall pass through the clouds in the bluish atmosphere. He shall move like the most majestic bird, coming to rest in an empty chair in the chambers of the sun-king. Soon he shall navigate in this ship toward heaven, since he shall guide the rudder. Oh all-powerful sun-god, the imperishable spirit of King Unas is coming to you! Receive your son so that you can traverse the celestial route together, united in the shadows, and appear wherever you wish at some place on the horizon!

This type of prayer to a god could at times become a warning to an enemy. This gives us the notion of serious threats that weighed on Egyptian civilisation. With time, there were so many that they ended up destroying it. This is why it became necessary to threaten bitter enemies using phrases such as these:

"King Unas is so powerful that he devours those who attempt to threaten him, since he lives alongside the kings. He has many serfs who await his orders to attack. Among these are the head hunters, who are ready to capture careless ones. The snake with the raised head also keeps watch so that no threats may awaken him, and that which "is found on the red of blood" (heri-terut) is ready to put you in chains. Khonsu kills the enemy captains; he slits their throats and takes out their entrails to defend King Unas. The squeezing-king dismembers them so that King Unas can bake them in his oven for dinner.

King Unas himself eats their magic virtues and transfigured souls. The largest ones are served to him in the morning, the average ones at midday, and the small ones in the evening. The elderly are used for light in his home. The north stars illuminate the fire under his cauldrons with the buttocks of the oldest ones. The inhabitants of heaven kneel before King Unas in order to pay homage to him when the feet of their wives burn in his home...

However, these hieroglyphics could not be read by the enemies, so they remained in the burial chambers as invocations, just as if the desire to eliminate the threat could act as an evil spell. Egypt did not only create the most fabulous things, but it also lived in a very special world, an immense fable, as is proven by reading the "Book of the Dead" and the knowledge about their relationship with the gods. There is a reason why it was a magical, hermetic civilisation, why the most trivial deed must be viewed as a reality born from the divine.

A brief comment on the Pyramids

The Egyptian Pyramids were originally surrounded by quadrangular walls, and they were accompanied by other, smaller or auxiliary pyramids, whose purpose is still not clear. We must remember, however, that these lesser pyramids never served as tombs. Were they perhaps a way of distracting potential despoilers?

Different temples were placed inside the rectangle, in which different ceremonies were held. All of them had underground galleries which led to chambers where the pharaohs were buried. On some occasions a covered path was built, which was called the 'Royal Passageway', and which united the pyramid to the 'Temple of the Valley', where the most important ceremonies were held.

Chapter III

MAGIC AND RELIGION

The cradle of the magic of the Mediterranean

In Plutarch's book "Isis and Osiris", one can read: *The sphinxes that the Egyptians placed before their temples tell us that the essence of their holy doctrine forms part of that which is mysterious...* And for more than forty centuries the arid plains where the pharaohs' pyramids were built have remained, just like sleeping giants made of stone, like jealous guardians of the most valuable secrets and mysteries about life and death.

They also assume the arts that decipher the nature of things, since they allow living human beings to establish indirect communication with the gods and the dead. This is why other civilisations took the science of the 'beyond' from Egypt; their belief that there existed a direct relationship between heaven and earth. That is how Greece and Rome learnt these lessons. Even the Jews viewed the nation of the pyramids as the cradle of secrets worth inheriting. This is why in the Hebrew 'Talmud', one can read, referring to Christ, *he had been initiated into the mysteries of Egypt.* This is how they justified the fact that he was able to heal the ill and revive the dead. Even in times closer to ours, such as the Middle Ages, alchemists felt an irresistible fascination with everything about Egypt and the pyramids. And were not occultists from the eighteenth century, such as Cagliostro and Count Saint-Germain, considered sons of Egypt and connoisseurs of its great secrets? In the current state of research on the Occult Sciences, no one dares to question the fact that Egypt is the cradle of the magic of the Mediterranean countries.

The dead one could become a god, or...

Just as happened in other ancient civilisations, Egyptian beliefs governed their magical practices; furthermore, the majority of these practices were religious, yet they always demonstrated a great deal of realism. The priest's gestures and words had to do a specific thing, either in the physical or psychological realm. Depending on the formula used, the god had to respond in order to provide a clearly-defined favour. Careful they don't trick you!

There were terrible spells that, when spoken by a magician, ended up arriving at the mentioned god in a violent or cruel way. Indeed, the magician or priest was convinced that he could threaten the divinity, whether in his own name or in that of his clients. For example, he would shout:

"If you do not bring the boat to the shore where he is, I shall pull out the curls from your head as if they were mere flower buds!"

If a favour had not been granted to a dead person, the magician invoked lightning, so that it could strike the arm of Shou, who held up the vaults of heaven. The gods were also threatened with being robbed of their pieces of meat that had been left on their altars, just as they were warned that they would not receive any further offerings if they continued to refuse the requested favour.

Such demanding invocations could come from the mouth of a pharaoh, such as Ramses II, who when he saw himself surrounded by two thousand five hundred enemy chariots, invoked the help of Amon, his father-god, mentioning the many gifts he had given him for which he must be grateful and must help him gain victory, even though the situation was so dangerous for him and his army.

These religious practices were multiplied at the moment of death. He who was to be embalmed in accordance with the holy rules and have the most advantageous amulets did not fear the passage to the 'beyond' since he was sure that his new life would be rich and rewarding.

The impressive "Book of the Dead" was left alongside the mummy or under his head. It could also be transcribed on his bandages or on the walls of the tomb. Thanks to the magical incantations it contained, the deceased would be able to vanquish the monsters that would attempt to prevent him from crossing the twenty-one pillars, the fifteen gates and the seven rooms in order to reach the forty-two judges. The "Book of the Dead" also indicated the magic name of the gods and the way to ask for their pardon. The obligatory message was something like this: *I did nothing of which you accuse me.*

Nevertheless, a negative confession was not enough to satisfy the judges. Before they decided if the dead person had been worthy of the honour of becoming a god, becoming equal to Osiris, or being turned over to the infernal monsters, he had to submit to a ceremony called 'weigh the heart'. But the priest-magician continued to intervene, once again threatening the gods violently:

If my protected one does not receive the satisfaction he deserves, I shall make it so that Ra can never rise to heaven, because I shall throw him into the Nile, where he shall live with the fish!

This was a dialogue between equals, because the dead person's right to become a god was being defended, thus making him equal to the most important divinity in the Egyptian heaven. This is a surprising way to view religion and does not occur in the Judeo-Christian religions, in which the one God deserves to be treated with respect, and whomever invokes his name does so as a penitent, that is, as an inferior being.

The theory of 'ba' and 'ka'

The Egyptians surrounded death with a metaphysical concept, which was like a magical element. They believed in the theory of 'ba' and 'ka'. In their concept of the immortality of the soul, they made a distinction between 'ba' and 'ka'. The former was the soul, which was represented by the shape of a hawk with a human head that left the body at the time of earthly death to travel to the other world, where it would live in the private dominions of the divinity to which it had been consecrated.

Once the deceased had been deposited in the tomb, their double, or 'ka', could enjoy a magical existence amidst familiar objects or their representations engraved on the stone, drilled into the wood, painted on porcelain or shaped into images. This is why the burial chambers that have been found inside the pyramids are full of objects, those which it was assumed the 'ka' of the deceased person would enjoy. On some occasions, all the objects in a household were included, as has been seen in different excavations, and we can see that the different underground chambers reproduced with great exactness the contents of an important man's home, with all its furniture, objects, mummified domesticated animals and even food.

However, on occasions it was not necessary to formulate a real offering in order to aid the existence of the double, or 'ka'. It was enough to utter, in honour of the dead, a ritual's formula in order to ensure that the double would possess the objects that were to be placed alongside the coffin.

Can we provide an exact idea of what the Egyptians called 'ka'? In one of the scenes engraved on the walls of the temple of Luxor, one can see that Khum, the potter-god, is shaping two exactly similar human forms, which would end up being enclosed inside Queen Ahmose. One of them represents the physical form, so it has the appearance of the flesh, while the other is the fluid material (the 'ka'), which will exist throughout life inside the being made of flesh and bone, whom it shall accompany in its normal development, since the double is always born and grows with the human body.

Precisely this 'ka', the double of the Egyptians, in some way represented (in so far as one can be precise on this matter) the fluid essence of the body to which it belonged. It has also apparently been considered the repository of the individual's psychic energies, since in certain magical practices, such as witchcraft, the witch's 'ka' took possession of the bewitched person's 'ka'.

In the same way, death was attributed to the fact that the 'ka' left the body. With the passage of time, 'ka' became equated with consciousness: the devil that dwelt in the human body. At the moment of death, the 'ka' released from the body transformed into a ghost, which kept its consciousness but was separated from its divine elements (soul and spirit), which had reached the celestial regions. The Egyptians believed that this would not prevent the soul from momentarily uniting with its 'ka' during the magical invocation ceremonies in order to teach priests about the things that happened in the beyond, as if the 'ka' were acting as a type of medium.

Amulets were also used to protect the mummy against bad spirits, rodents and those who would desecrate the tombs. For this reason an inscription could be read:

I am the kher-heb (the lector priest) materialised, this is why I know all the secrets. This meant that the dead person knew the most fearsome knowledge, meaning that he could revenge whoever damaged his tomb. To this another somewhat mysterious phrase was added: *I will be like the crocodile when something breaks the calm of the water where it rests or like the snake that is awoken from its best dreams...* This might mean that vengeance would pursue the desecrator for many years, killing him when he least expected it. It is possible that the threatening invocation led to curses, such as those that hounded and killed whoever dared to 'interrupt the eternal sleep' of Tutankhamen.

Since it was necessary that no outsider enter the tombs, consequently destroying the magical atmosphere created by the ritual action of the kher-heb (the lector priest or the "scribe of god"), these curses were created. All of them came from the ceremony of the 'sa', which was the fluid that gave the dead person an ineffable, eternal existence that was impossible for other mortals to see.

The priest transmitted the 'sa' through certain magical movements over the deceased person's neck and back. The priest, in turn, had received this ability from the wisest of his predecessors. All pharaohs, being the sons of Ra, the sun-god, would receive it from his father. From this moment on he could transmit it or take advantage of it himself.

The fear that a desecrator would break the magical charm of the tombs led them to build almost impassable barriers inside the pyramids. The fact that the mummies were accompanied by infinite riches would pose such an irresistible temptation; that was why the threats were engraved or painted on the walls using hieroglyphics, with those labyrinths that had taken almost forty centuries to be defeated, although some of them still haven't been desecrated. But one day they will not be able to resist either.

The speaking statues

The Egyptians were convinced that if the corpse were destroyed, it would be quite easy to replace it so that the 'ka' could continue to exist through an image that was as similar as possible to the deceased person. This was the purpose of the majority of statues found inside the tombs. All the statues were placed inside special chambers within the pyramids.

However, since in Egypt any magical practice required its own ritual, the statue was also subjected to 'sa' in order for it to be able to support the 'ka'. This is why it was left on top of a small mound of sand, which was like a funerary mountain, in order to subject it to the influence of the mummy. They made it hold the magical sceptre, which was a snake head and a three-tailed whip, and at the same time had to lean against the 'naos' or arc into which the corpse had been put. At this time, the dead person's fluid began to surround the statue, with the neck as the starting point.

The magician-priests were convinced that by using magical statues they could establish contact with the spirit of the dead person or the god, since it had been converted into the best holders of the 'ka'. This was the first step leading to the speaking statues, some of whose speeches were recorded on papyrus. In accordance with what is stated on Egyptian papyrus, we have learned that the pharaoh's court or the entire people were enraptured witnesses of such divine manifestations, a wonder that took place between the magician-priests and the gods.

As an example, we shall cite what happened to Queen Hatshepsut during one ceremony. Suddenly the statue of Amon came down from its pedestal, walked around the great hall and stopped before a young man who would later be Tuthmosis III. On another occasion, the victim of a robbery spoke to the statue in order to discover the thief. Shortly thereafter, in a procession, the statue indicated with a head movement where the thief was hiding. The thief was not found there, but all the loot was, even though it was very well hidden.

As a third example, we shall mention what happened to a worker who was suing a neighbour for the ownership of a house. When he spoke to the statue, the worker exclaimed: *Come to my aid, my great Sun!* The statue resolved the conflict with a movement of its head, supporting the reasoning of the man who had just invoked him.

The most famous event involving a speaking statue comes from the year 332 BC. It features Alexander the Great. It seems that on the Siwa Oasis there was an oracle of Amon who was very well known throughout the East and Greece. Since Alexander had just conquered the Egyptians and then made them name him pharaoh under the name of Meryamun Setepenra Aleksandros, he decided to go to this place in order to find out his destiny. Amon only responded in writing; nevertheless, before such an important interlocutor, he decided to speak:

"Do you grant me the right to possess the entire world?" Alexander asked him.

"Yes," responded the god.

Then the great conqueror asked the divinity about his father's murder.

"Has one of my father's assassins escaped my vengeance?"

"Do not blaspheme. No mortal can go against your father."

The god's response can be better understood if we are aware that only the descendants of the pharaohs, that is, the dynasty of the gods, could occupy the throne of Egypt. Thus

33

it was told that Alexander the Great, despite being the puta-
tive son of Phillip, the son of Nectanebo, the dethroned
pharaoh who had later engendered him after pouring a love
potion on Olympia and entering the bed in the form of a ser-
pent. This meant that Alexander was the son of a pharaoh,
thus a god who had nothing to fear from mortals. The oracle
of Amon simply confirmed the legend.

In all ages there have been researchers who have been
very sceptical about the speaking statues. The same goes for
many Egyptologists, who explain the phenomenon as tricks
by ventriloquist priests or people who pushed springs. But
current parapsychologists say that these might be the first
known cases of mediums, that is, that the statues became
transmitters of the voices of the dead.

The magical power of the word

The Egyptians believed that nothing could exist if it had
been uttered. This is why the god Thot personified the tongue.
In order for human beings, irrational beings and things to
have a real existence, they had to be uttered or 'projected
from the inside out' by those who had conceived them.

According to what has been read in the hieroglyphic
inscriptions, *the tongue creates everything that loves and at
the same time everything that hates; the tongue is the creator
of everything that exists. Nothing can live if it had not first
been uttered aloud.* Thus, such great importance was placed
on spoken rituals in Egypt. As is logical, this belief gave great
importance to names. The name formed an integral part of the
'ka' of the person to which it belonged and was, to some
degree, its spiritual synthesis.

Pharaoh was god

When god said to the pharaoh: *You are the son of my stomach;* we do not need to view this as figurative in meaning. The
Egyptians had developed a very concrete concept of the mystery of incarnation. The union of the god and the queen is rep-

resented on the walls in the temples of Deir el Bahari and Luxor. The pharaoh received from god the magical fluid through the ceremony of 'sa'. Thus everything in his person was magical. His crown, the 'pshent', was made by the union of the red crown of the north and the white crown of the south, given the name of the 'great bewitcher'. A circle, the 'uraeus' or 'great charmer', was mounted on its base, giving off flames and reaching the enemies.

The two ram's horns which literally sprang from the base of the crown symbolised the conducting poles of the beneficent or terrible light that causes life or death. The sceptre of the pharaoh was also magical; it offered existence. The three-tailed whip gave off the magic fluid and also frightened the evil spirits. The white stone mace was not only used to kill victims, since with this final sacrifice it also enabled them to acquire the dignity needed to be offered to the gods, as if in a type of consecration.

The pharaoh also possessed the magical gift of yelling with the voice of the magicians. Ramses II showed his family during one council the disadvantages of the lack of potable water along the Nubian paths that led to the gold mines. This had led to the death of many caravan drivers and their asses. Then one of his councillors reminded him of his power:

"You are identical to Ra in everything you do; consequently, there is no doubt that your heart's desires will come true. If you desire something during the night, at daybreak it will already be done. If you say to the water: go to the mountain, the waters of heaven will immediately spring at the call of your voice because you are the incarnation of Ra!"

We know that while he governed a council, Ramses was in permanent contact with the gods. He also maintained a continuous dialogue with them through religious ceremonies. There was a formula for the majority of questions that could be posed to a certain god. Generally speaking, the pharaoh invoked his aid against enemies, whether divine or mortal. But this help had to be reciprocal.

If the pharaoh requested services, he had to provide other services in return, since this ceremony was rarely limited to covering ritualised formulas. For example, Queen Hatshepsut, from the eighteenth dynasty, was thinking about building Deir-el-Bahari in 1450 BC. Thus upon entering a temple she could immediately hear the lord of the gods himself order her to go up the paths of the Punt, to take the paths that would lead to the 'Steps of Incense', where communication between the two would be better.

As we can see, the dialogue between gods and Egyptian monarchs was direct. But it was not just about asking for advice or exchanging promises. During combat, if the outcome seemed doubtful it was believed that Ra occupied a place in the same chariot next to the pharaoh. On seeing himself being abandoned by his soldiers, Ramses II, from the nineteenth dynasty, invoked the help of his father, Amon-Ra. And the god came to help his son, to whom he cried:

"Elbow to elbow with you! My strength is your strength! Ramses-Meryamun, I have come to help you! I am your father! My hand is yours, because together we are worth more than one hundred thousand of your men! I, the strong one, who loves bravery, have seen a brave heart in you, and I am very satisfied! Now our will shall be done!"

We know that the enemies were exterminated. Later, peace was signed in accordance with the conditions set forth by the god himself.

Under the eighteenth dynasty, during the time when the priestly caste dominated, the pharaoh never acted alone when he was consulting the gods. He had to refer to the statue of Amon, who approved or disapproved, always in public, the decrees read by the head priest. The divine statue's decisions were indicated by movements of its head.

The magical defence of buildings

The priests were in charge of the magical defence of the buildings against malign beings. To do so they ensured the purity of the ground, the influence of its owner, the opportune nature of the day and time chosen to begin building and the building's orientation. Thus, when building a temple they chose the sixth day of the month and the earliest morning hours, and the site was then purified. The pharaoh himself or, in his absence, the head priest, would be entrusted with such an important mission.

The ceremony began with the offering of sacrifices to the gods. Once the building was finished, amulets were hung, magical formulas were engraved and statues or sphinxes were installed. For greater security, the temple had to be protected by a snake, whether figurative or real, as a reminder of 'uraeus'. With this sphinx, the entrance was protected, and it was accompanied by the use of heavy doors and solid locks. Obelisks, poles and pylons were also used for defence.

The temples of the gods were not the only buildings with magical defences. In the British Museum, there is a papyrus from the twenty-second dynasty which mentions the protection of the royal treasure. The scribe wrote it in the name of Osiris *for the place where the treasure shall go. This hidden book shall defeat evil curses and destroy thieves, because life and death come from it.*

Houses were also magically defended. In a manuscript from the Saite Era we can read this invocation addressed to the goddess Neith, with the purpose of protecting against attacks by poisonous reptiles and insects:

Enter our house, oh Neith, in which Osiris N is located (this must have been a home in which a mummy in a burial cell was kept), close the mouth of all snakes, both male and female, and scorpions so that they do not enter where they are not wanted.

This formula had to be accompanied by the entire space being sprinkled with the essence of certain plants. Finally, the plants themselves or their remains were left in the inside corners.

Certain "pyramidologists" theory is even more curious. They claim that the Great Pyramid (referring to that of Cheops, built in the year 3000 BC) was raised with the intention of guarding a message in which the dates of great future events can be found, prophecies of which we shall speak in more detail further on. The way in which the 'passageways' are organised and the dates, predict some very important events. Thus, this speaking stone would have foretold:

1st. The advent of Jesus Christ.
2nd. His death.
3rd. The First World War in 1914.
4th. Peace from 1918 to 1928.
5th. The economic crisis of 1928 to 1936.
6th. A period of war disturbances from 1936 to 1953...

Non-priestly magic

If the pharaohs and priests could speak with the gods, mere mortals could also attempt it in an indirect way. This is why the life of the Egyptian people was full of magic, both black and white. The worship of the dead and the gods played a prominent role in daily life, allowing people to come closer to the 'beyond'.

This made Egypt the magical land *par excellence*. We can see this in the fact that it was believed that living beings and things had a double life, a hidden power. Behind visible objects, the Egyptians' imaginations had created an entire mysterious world whose spirit was in the essence of the wind, the movements of the leaves and natural life; full of mysterious signs and messages.

Long before the pyramids were built, there were already magicians. All of them possessed necromantic powers since they knew the secrets of establishing contact with the dead. They were also prophets, healers and witches. One of their rituals was called the 'antoninus'. As is described in a papyrus series, all of which are found in the British Museum and the Leyden Museum, we can see that this magic was taught in the 'House of Life'. The books they studied in this building were ancient and had been written by the gods.

Education was quite complicated since it was not enough to merely recite a formula or make a magical gesture if an immediate result was desired. It was necessary to submit to periods of purification and long, painstaking preparations. For example, if one wished to ensure 'a person's happiness', a nine-day purification, anointing using special oils, carefully washing the mouth with natron, making ablutions with water from 'the flood' (this indicates to us that this could only be done during certain times of the year when the Nile was in flood), wearing white leather sandals and putting on new linen smocks which had been sprinkled with incense were necessary. Then a feather was drawn on the tongue with green ink, symbolising the truth. Finally, a circle was drawn using the colour pertaining to the god of this day (one of the seven sacred colours).

When one wanted to stop an enemy's action, the following procedure was used: one had to have an ass' head (symbol of Seth), scrub one's feet with clay and then place oneself before the sun, keeping the bleeding ass' head between one's legs. After having scrubbed one's hands and feet with this same blood, one extended one's arm forward, leaving the hand open, while extending other arm backward. Then the magical formula invoking Seth-Typhon had to be uttered: *You, the terrible one, the invincible one, the all-powerful one, the god of gods, the corrupter and devastator! You whose nickname is he who destroys everything and who was never beaten!*

Another formula for a spell consisted in sealing the mouth or arms and legs of a wax statue. The virgin wax was made to run while the imprecatory formulas were spoken over the mouth in order to paralyse the murmuring tongue. The procedure was the same in order to paralyse any of the upper or lower extremities of a potential enemy.

Amulets, talismans and other magical elements

The selling of amulets, talismans and other magical elements was a true business for the priests. They sold necklaces and bracelets to those who had transmitted the 'sa' through magnetic spells. Some of these objects were engraved with witchcraft formulas. They also offered talismans in the form of hieroglyphs, which might represent what their future owner needed: bodily and spiritual youth (symbolised by a lettuce leaf), economic stability (an image of four columns) or power (the sceptre).

The jewellery materials that the priests purveyed had their own virtues: gold, as a royal metal, gave the greatest advantages. Colours, too, held great meaning. For example, green represented health and thus gave good health. If an Egyptian hung a tablet made of magic wood around his neck, he knew that he was protected from the 'evil eye'. A cord with seven knots, which had been tied while uttering the required spells, permanently 'tied up' the seven malign genies of the days of the week. A skein of tow forced harmful spirits to count these threads before attaching the person wearing them. One of the protective formulas referred to certain spells which required the use of various ingredients, all of which had their own unique magical properties, as we shall see below.

In the waning years of Egyptian civilisation, amulets and talismans were replaced by gems. Small images of gods and mysterious words were engraved on these precious stones. They were usually worn on the fingers of the right hand. Furthermore, Egyptian magicians made extensive use of herbs. With them, they would make love potions, short- or long-term poisons, medicines, and they even used them to read the future. In these cases they also used a child to act as a seer. They placed him in front of a new oil lamp, over whose flame he had to focus his sight. Then the magician began to utter the ritual invocations, and he regularly threw handfuls of magical herbs into the fire. As the child fell into a hypnotic state from staring so closely at the flame and as a result of the smoke that was burning, he began to reveal the future depending on the questions asked.

Egyptian priests used many divining tools: staring into a glass mirror; shaking rings placed in a row onto a small bar and hung over a tripod, where magical herbs were burning; divining consequences based on the direction of the smoke produced by the head of an ass when it was toasted among embers; observing the images that formed in the bottom of a cup full of water; making arithmetical calculations which when interpreted by special rules gave answers to the questions that had been asked; and so forth.

The interpretation of dreams

The "Book of Dreams", written during the New Empire, mentions dream interpretation, which is in fashion in the West today. For example: *he who sees himself dead shall have a long life; he who dreams that his teeth are falling out, will soon lose a family member; he who sees himself in a mirror, poor thing, because this means he will have a second wife; he who sees himself throwing himself into a well, shall find what he seeks.*

Perhaps Egypt's divining tools, which, all magical, are surprising. Each of them is very useful for attacking, defending or protecting what one loves. But was this entire land populated by invisible beings, genies, ghosts and malign spirits constantly attempting to suck the blood from the living, to transform themselves into ferocious beasts to devour or bite poor travellers or drive human beings crazy by taking possession of their 'ka'?

In order to defend itself from all this, Egypt had a powerful tool, which shall be dealt with in the following chapter.

The most ancient medicine

A medical papyrus from the Hiksos period was found in Thebes by Edwin Smith but published by J. H. Breadsted in his book "Chronicle of Egypt", contains the most ancient treatise on pathological medicine in the world. It is highly scientific, although it is accompanied by a great many magical formulas.

Since the Egyptians attributed all phenomena to supernatural causes, we should not be surprised that they saw ill people as victims of the gods' ire, or the 'ka' of certain men. Thus, it was necessary to send the 'ka' of the god or the man who had 'possessed' the patient very far away.

To accomplish this, magnetic exorcisms were used. If the rites were ineffective, they then proceeded to administer medicines. A large number of these medicines were part of an official pharmacopoeia, while others were created in an exclusively magical, secret way: herbs chosen in accordance with rituals that few knew about, gathered on special days and at special times, and also had to be cooked in new vessels on which magical formulas had been engraved. In addition, the product was subjected to the action of the moon and the planets and finally to the magical effect of movements made with magnets near three oil lamps.

The magical defence formulas were those that provided the antidote to all possible illnesses. Next to their child's cradle, many mothers repeated the magical words meant to keep illness at bay, which the kiss of 'ka' might have secreted onto the child's body:

Disappear, death that comes from the shadows, who has entered stealthily with its nose crushed and twisted by your mask! Disappear, without leaving the evil that you bring! If you have come to kiss him, I shall not allow it; nor to mark him; nor to take him from me, nor to soothe him! I have made spells against you with the lettuce that is born, garlic that causes much harm, with the honey which is sweet to man but repugnant to the dead, and with the backbone of the latus (a Nile fish)*!*

And this other one, whose efficacy if perhaps more doubtful and is not lacking in poetry, was sung in order to protect the child who was still in his mother's womb:

Oh my little bird! Are you warm in your nest? Your mother is with you, but you do not have a sister to fan you or a wet nurse to coddle you! Let them bring me long golden pearls, round amethyst beads, a stone seal engraved with a crocodile and a hand (a symbol of protection) *to deflect and reject that which takes pleasure in burning innocents! Disappear before this spell, evil enemy!*

Defence against death

When the magician-priest wanted to keep the person under his protection alive, he began to enumerate the seventy-seven types of death, and then he said:

Disappear, ill-fated agent, who wishes to be the one to penetrate a body that does not yet belong to it! If the male or female enemy of this part (at which point the priest touched the ill part), *if the mortal germs, whoever they may be, take long to be destroyed, may heaven be divided! May the earth revolve! May Apophis* (the snake that fought against the sun) *remain in the solar ship for millions of years; may water not be provided to the one in the ship* (referring to Osiris); *may he who is in Abydos* (Osiris once again) *never be entombed!*

After this series of ill wishes to the gods, the magician-priest proceeded to the specific part of the threat:

May humans no longer present offerings at any of the festivals of the divinities who refuse to protect them!

If the gods ended up saving the ill person, things would go much better for everyone, since the offerings would continue to adorn their altars. If not, as rarely happened, the family members of the deceased person would not appeal to the gods for many years.

We can now skip to the period of the Greeks, whose medicinal practises we are more familiar with. For example, we know that crazy people were considered possessed and were enclosed in the temple grounds so that the gods could release them from their demons. The secret science of the sacred herbs was discovered by Imhotep himself, who in his temple revealed it to the Greek doctor, Thessalos, as well as telling them *the most propitious times and places for gathering these plants*. Eye diseases in Egypt were attributed to both Isis and the astral gods, since the sun acted on the right eye while the moon acted on the left.

The influence of the nebulas was also considered harmful; since they were formed by barely visible stars they could produce vision problems. This proves to us that astrology already had begun to govern medicine. Dream interpretation also had an influence: patients could have their dreams interpreted in the temples of the healing gods, especially in that of Imhotep. These dreams duly monitored by the dream interpreter, who knew how to discern deceptive dreams from real appearances, also provided medicinal indications.

On occasions, the magician-priest would even evoke the soul of a dead person or a god in order for him to directly council the ill person from the beyond as to the treatment to be followed. This was the period when necromancy did not form part of the secret art of the temples, and the end of Egypt's mysterious period was near.

Alchemy and astrology

The Egyptians were great artists and even better artisans, but they also left us bountiful testimony of their skills as chemists. They had special procedures for colouring precious stones, enamel, cameos, porcelain and other materials. It is also known that they knew the secret to imitating all the precious stones and even pearls.

In contrast, there is no doubt that the formulas used by chemists in the Middle Ages, those that were used to transform metals, had been passed down from Hermes Trismegisto, an Egyptian god who was identified with Thot, Ptah and Khnum. Some manuscripts preserved in the museums at Leyden and Stockholm, specifically deal with the purification of lead and tin, the transformation of this metal into silver, the bleaching of copper, the way of folding gold, manufacturing bullion, and, according to Lepsius, electrum (an alloy of gold and silver). For the last one, alum and salt from Cappadocia were used. But these documents, the majority of them written in Greek and dating from the first few centuries AD, cannot provide evidence that alchemy had been an ancient, widely practised science in Egypt.

With regard to astrology, especially divinatory astrology, which would later be called 'judicial astrology', it appears that the Egypt of the great national periods paid little attention to it, judging by the highly limited number of horoscopes that have been discovered, some of which were transcribed on papyrus dating from the twentieth dynasty, preserved in the museum of Egyptology in the Italian city of Turin.

Nevertheless, nothing prevents us from assuming that one day a more conclusive document will be found, due to the fact that Egypt was the land of surprises, as proven by M. W. Gundel's find, consisting of a Renaissance manuscript, the *Liber Hermetis*, which also dealt with Egyptian astrology, in which the translation of a Greek work from the Alexandrian period is acknowledged, some of whose parts date from the third century BC.

This manuscript provides authentic revelations in Greco-Egyptian astrology, leading us to admit that the Egyptian priests played a more important role than was acknowledged until today in the development of this pseudo-science, while also bringing a more independent originality from the Chaldean masters, of whom these masters had previously been disciples.

In any event, we are dealing with Egypt's period of decline, although this document might refer to a more ancient science, as commentator M. W. Gundel attempts to demonstrate. Despite the importance they might have, it is indisputable that the Egyptians, even those from the earliest dynasties, were always concerned with heavenly matters. Indeed, did the god Thot not teach humans philosophy and astronomy? It even becomes incontrovertible, as indicated by some prescriptions, that the magician-priests always kept in mind astral influences when developing and administering medicines, just as they must have used them in all magical acts.

However, it appears that they kept the secret of this branch of their science, since the calendars of the good and evil days that we have, one from the Middle Empire and the other from the New Empire, were exclusively based on the anniversaries of the deeds related to the gods and make no allusion to astral influences. For example, one can read that the twelfth day of the first month of winter is very evil, such that one should avoid seeing a mouse in this time since it corresponds to the moment in which he (Ra) has ordered Sekhmet to exterminate the human race. With regard to the first day of the fourth month of winter, *which always is very good and during which a great festival is held in heaven and on earth, this character is due to the fact that Sobek's enemies fell in their path on this day.* Thus, we must wait until the Greek period to witness the appearance of horoscopes and astrological priests, which made astral divination available to uninitiated people.

45

In this way, life in ancient Egypt seemed to have been bathed in occultism. From the pharaoh, son of god, to the man of the people, everyone looked toward the beyond to find the secret of relationships between human beings and the supernatural. Thus, it has seemed clear to some scholars that the proof of Egyptian magic is not as great as its extraordinary reputation as the 'land of the great secrets'. Durville and Doctor Mardrus have made special efforts to prove that the meaning of the "Book of the Dead" is beyond the understanding of the non-initiated. They present this religious work (and they maintain the same thesis with other holy books, especially the Jewish ones) as an initiation ritual in which everything is made symbolic in order to disguise the most important secrets.

Chapter IV

THE EGYPTIAN MUMMIES

The mummy suddenly sat up!

A corpse embalmed using the Egyptian techniques is called a mummy. These corpses were so well conserved within their funeral shrouds when they were 'unwrapped' that they appear to have been recently entombed.

Mummies have always been highly fascinating to westerners, and they even became terrifying due to an event that took place at the beginning of the twentieth century. The mummy of Ramses II, one of the most powerful Egyptian monarchs who conquered the entire Middle East, had been deposited at the Cairo Museum.

It was a warm, humid day. The visitors to the Museum had stopped to look at the dried, wizened body, when... Suddenly the mummy sat up! It did more than that: it broke the urn that covered it with its hand and sat upright!

The visitors might not have actually see this, since they had left running, terrified by the fact that a corpse that had supposedly been 'sleeping' for more than 3,300 years, had 'come alive'. It was quite difficult to calm the newspaper readers, despite the fact that the doctors explained the phenomenon: certain corpses experience sudden dilation of their tissues when subjected to a brusque change in temperature. The mummy came from the Valley of the Kings, in the Thebes desert, where it had never rained, while in the museum the atmosphere was humid and cooler, and this had caused the spectacle.

But many people did not believe this explanation, while others, the canniest ones, converted it into a plot for their novels. This is how the terrifying myth of the 'living mummies', so often exploited in theatre, films, television and popular literature, came about. It is a terrifying tradition, whose 'commercial' products could fill an entire library.

The curse of the mummies

Not all mummies were equal, nor were they prepared in the same way. During the earliest dynasties of the pharaohs, around 2,700 BC, they took care to keep a plaster cast of the corpses in order to preserve their main characteristics. It was the builders of the pyramids, continually preoccupied with ensuring their immortality, who improved the process.

We are talking about the kings of the third and fourth dynasties, that is, around 2,600 BC. At first this privilege was reserved for the pharaohs. It is believed that Cheops' great frustration when he found out that his mother's sepulchre had been violated, along with seeing the disintegrated body, led him to improve the embalming techniques, perhaps while the Great Pyramid that bears his name was being built.

It is well known that the mummy of Menkaure was embalmed in this way, proven when it arrived in England in the nineteenth century. His is considered the 'first' mummy. Curiously, it took some time before it could be deposited in the British Museum since the ship that was transporting it sank along the Spanish coasts in a storm, an event that many blame on the 'curse of the pharaohs', despite the fact that when the royal sarcophagus was rescued, it was taken to its destination, without 'suffering' any further accidents.

An honour that could be proven

In the eleventh dynasty (2,000 BC), many advances took place with regard to who could be mummified. Now, all the members of the Egyptian nobility had this honour, in addition to the pharaohs and head priests. Soon anyone who could afford it could be mummified, as long as he was not a criminal or an acknowledged sinner.

Economic well-being, as well as a long period of peace, made many families wealthy, feeding their desire to be immortalised. This time of prosperity might have arisen when the Nile was channelled at certain parts of its course.

At the same time, the embalming techniques were improved. The corpse's intestines were extracted and then the empty spaces were filled with very expensive cloths which had previously been treated so that they would not rot. Throughout the eighteenth dynasty (1,400 BC), 'anyone' could buy their own mummification as long as they had enough money to afford the honour. The vanity of some of the 'bourgeoisie' led them to request that instead of just their eyes, their entire corpses were encrusted with very expensive crystals or precious stones.

Herodotus' testimony

When the most important Greek travellers began to reach Egypt, especially after Alexander the Great had conquered it in 330 BC, they focused their attention on the mummies and their embalming process. This is precisely what Herodotus of Halicarnassus did. He wrote about it in the II Book of History as follows:

85. The funerary cries and burial take place in the following way: whenever a man of a certain social status dies in a household, all the women in the family cover their heads, and sometimes even their faces, in mud. Once they have left the corpse in the bed, they go through the city in their undergarments with their breasts exposed, hitting themselves. All women who have any type of relationship with the dead man do this. For their part, the men also hit their bodies after stripping down to their undergarments. Finally, the dead person is taken to be embalmed.

86. The specialists who devote themselves to the art of embalming wait there. When a corpse is brought to their houses, they show those who brought it wooden figures as proof of what they can offer, since due to their colours and forms they seem like living bodies sleeping most peacefully. The best of these figures is that of a being whose name I dare not say (he is referring to Osiris). *They then show a cheaper figure of lesser quality, and a third, even cheaper than the others. They then ask which one the family wants for the deceased person. As soon as the price is negotiated, the embalmer receives the corpse.*

Once he is alone in his workshop, he begins to perform a masterly job. He introduces curved irons into the corpse's nose and after extracting the brains he puts drugs and ingredients only known by his counterparts into the cavity. He then opens the deceased person's flanks with a very sharp stone from Ethiopia in order to take out the intestines, clean out the stomach and wash it with palm wine and ground aromas. Finally, he fills it with myrrh, cassia and all types of perfumes, with the exception of incense. In this way the body is ready to be sewn closed, which is done with great precision.

The next process is putting the corpse into a tanning mixture, in which it is left with natron for sixty days. It is then wrapped, after having washed it painstakingly. He uses very fine linen strips which he spreads with rubber, used by Egyptians as glue. After another sixty days, the dead person's family arrives, they take the mummy and they put it into a wooden box in the shape of a human body. They usually set it upright, supported on one of the main walls in the house.

Another way of preparing the corpse is used for those who do not wish for such luxury and regard. Without opening it, the embalming artists introduce cedar oil into the stomach of the dead person, filling it completely. Then they insert stoppers so that it does not leak out. They leave these corpses in the tanning mixture for the usual number of days, and finally, they let the oil out. It spurts out violently, bringing with it the intestines and entrails which have liquefied if not dissolved. The flesh is consumed by the nitre bath. Only skin and bones remain of the corpse. Without taking any further steps, the mummy is turned over to its family, who seem quite satisfied with the job.

The third method, which was used by the 'poorest' customers, consisted in emptying the corpse by using enemas. It was then tanned for the established period of time and finally turned over to the family members who had brought it. Herodotus also told what was done with the corpses of women and certain very important foreigners:

88. Nevertheless, with the wives of notable men, embalming did not take place right away and even less so if they were beautiful and important. They preferred to wait four or five days, when the body began to rot, with the sole reason of ensuring that the specialists in charge of mummification would not rape them. Indeed, some of them had been surprised and denounced by their own colleagues while copulating with a recently deceased female corpse.

89. If an Egyptian, or even a foreigner, had died trapped by a crocodile or drowned in a river, the city to which it had been brought was absolutely obliged to embalm and adorn it. It would do so in the most costly and dignified way, and then bury it in a sacred coffin. Once in the coffin, not even its own family members could touch it. Only the priests of the Nile were allowed to touch its hands, since with this burial it had become a supernatural being.

Was radiation used to mummify?

It has been calculated that in order to perform a perfect embalming, fifteen basic elements were needed, among them beeswax, with which all the orifices of the body and the eyes were plugged during the natron bath. Myrrh, cedar oil, palm rubber, onions, sawdust, fish, tar and natron were also used. Natron was a type of nitre salt which was gathered in the Negev and which the Egyptians used for cleaning.

Other products were used as well; however, we must especially bear in mind the almost permanent drought, the lack of humidity in the Egyptian desert, and the placement of the mummies underground, all of which considerably aided the marvellous conservation of these bodies.

Professor Ghoneim, who worked approximately thirty years ago in the Cairo Museum, as well as many modern

Egyptologists, claims that radiation was known in Egypt. The system used in the 1960s, especially in the United States, to irradiate agricultural waste in order to reduce the processes of putrefaction to the minimum while improving the methods for preserving food have been widely disseminated.

It is probable that on the shores of the Red Sea, some radioactive substances are found, the power of which as preservatives enable them to be used in some of the complicated embalming processes. Later we shall examine the effects of this theory in the famous affair, 'Tutankhamen's Curse'.

The golden masks

Families added necklaces, breastplates, amulets, bracelets, rings and sandals to the mummies. In addition, in the incision which the embalming artists had made in the corpse's stomach in order to extract the entrails, a small golden plaque was usually placed on which, the 'udjat' (magic eye), which cured wounds, was engraved. We have already mentioned that the "Book of the Dead" was also placed between the mummy's legs.

Furthermore, the corpse's body and face were covered with linen strips. Pharaohs, though, were also given a plaster mask of their face, painted with gold leaf. The golden mask found on Tutankhamen's mummy is considered to be one of the most beautiful goldsmith works in the entire history of art since it so closely resembles the mummy's face.

Before the final shrouding of the corpse, various sets of inscribed jewellery and tablets were placed on it. The last shroud was held in place by parallel bands. On some occasions, this was substituted by a type of cardboard box in the shape of the body, which the drawings found inside the sarcophagus were reproduced using gold and porcelain plates, as the finishing touches on a work of great beauty.

What was done with a pharaoh's entrails?

Could the entrails of a pharaoh who was considered a god have been thrown in the garbage? Impossible! This can be seen when examining Tutankhamen's tomb. Inside the tomb itself they placed a golden wood box which contained a chest with four compartments covered with the same number of alabaster figures, which were a repetition of the monarch's portrait. Miniature gold and crystal coffins incrusted with precious stones were extracted from the inside each compartment. Each of these sarcophagi contained parts of the pharaoh's intestines. The same was found in other tombs. The intestines of such important people, these gods, were conserved in golden and alabaster jars known as 'canopy cups'.

Tutankhamen did not deserve this mummy

On the 11th November, 1925, a team of eminent researchers of various nationalities met around Tutankhamen's mummy to proceed to examine it. Doctor Derry saw that the excess of ointments and perfumes that had been put on the mummy had harmed its preservation. Only its face and hands, which had been protected by gold pieces (the famous burial masks on the face and the pieces that covered the fingers and toes) had saved these parts from suffering such damage.

The rest of the body looked carbonised, as did the strips in which it was wrapped. Since the layer of ointments could not be taken off, they had to use a chisel. Under the head there was another surprise: an amulet in the shape of a crown... made of iron! It had always been believed that this metal was unknown to the Egyptian civilisation! How could this mystery be explained? Did it perhaps come from the Hittite king Shubiluliuma, with whom it seems they had signed a 'sphere of influence' treaty? Did it belong to the funeral goods of Tutankhamen's mother-in-law, Queen Nefertiti, whose unknown homeland might have been Syria, where they were already working with iron? We must understand that iron was humankind's secret weapon during the fourteenth century BC.

Returning to the mummy's side, we should add that it was very difficult to uncover the young pharaoh's features because the tissue had decomposed. But it was accomplished, since when it was cleaned it could be seen that it quite closely resembled the gold mask and the different portraits that had appeared in the tomb. More than one hundred groups of jewels had been taken from the body. So many objects were found that Doctor Carter needed thirty-three pages in his report to list them.

Tutankhamen's mummy's condition is thought to be among the worst of those found. This is why it remains in the Valley of the Kings, where tourists are not allowed to use cameras with flashbulbs to photograph it. We can see that this young monarch, who died when he was only eighteen years old, did not deserve this mummy, although this does not prevent him from being the most famous of all pharaohs, for another reason which we shall explain later.

The origin of mummy worship

It is believed that mummy worship had its origin in a legend which was part of the Egyptian religion. We do not know the beginning of this legend, but we do have various versions of it. We are referring to the myth of Osiris. He was the eldest son of the god of the Earth, Geb, and the goddess of the sky, Nut. He reigned in Egypt, teaching his subjects the arts, writing and agriculture. His brother, Seth, tried to kill him, using the following stratagem: he ordered a box to be built of the exact size of Osiris, who was a giant, and he ordered that he be taken to a banquet given in honour of his brother, who had returned from an expedition in faraway lands.

As soon as the banquet was over, when the joy of the reunion and the abundance of drinks had created the appropriate atmosphere, Seth promised an extraordinary gift to whoever dared to enter into the coffin and fill it completely. Many tried it, but only Osiris could meet the challenge. When he entered the box, Seth ordered it closed, and then his servants sent it down the Nile to its mouth, where they threw it into the sea.

Osiris' wife, the goddess Isis, patroness of magic and occult sciences, searched for him until she found his coffin in Byblos (Phoenicia), where it was protected by a very leafy tree. She brought it immediately to Egypt in order to resuscitate her husband using magical arts. When Ra, the sun-god, heard about this he sent the jackal Anubis, protector of the dead, to embalm Osiris' body. When it was ready, the goddess Isis extended her wings over her husband's corpse and resuscitated him. They then conceived a son, the god Horus, who is represented by a falcon, one of the figures that appear most often in Egyptian tombs.

Other legends tell that Seth found Osiris' corpse already embalmed before it came back to life. Thus he ordered that it be dismembered into sixteen pieces, which were then spread throughout Egypt. Isis recovered her husband's remains one by one, with the exception of one that had been taken to the Oxyrrinco River, where the fish devoured it. In order to take revenge, his son, Horus, confronted Seth. During the combat he lost an eye, but he won and then succeeded his father on the throne. Horus' magical eye was considered to be the protector of all sacrifices, and it was also believed that its presence ensured that funerary offerings would reach the other world in order to be collected by their proper beneficiaries. This is why it appears in almost all tombs.

Knowing these two legends from ancient Egypt, it is easy to understand the most powerful people's interest in mummifying their corpses. Furthermore, from the beginning Osiris was considered the god-king of the Kingdom of the Dead. Given the fact that the pharaohs were also considered gods, as the sons of the sun, they wanted to be identified with Osiris. This can be seen in thousands of inscriptions.

A burial ritual

One of the most important moments in a burial in the Theban age was the crossing of the Nile, from the 'shore of the living' (the current Luxor and Karnak) to the 'shore of the dead', where the Valley of the Kings is located. As they approached the tombs, the oxen were unyoked and the gigantic catafalque was dragged forward by the deceased person's friends and servants. Meanwhile, his wives and female servants cried incessantly, in the style of Arab and Hebrew mourners, which did not detract from the solemnity of the great event.

As soon as they arrived at the tomb, a special ceremony was held. The priest was in charge of cancelling the effects of the embalming in order to give elasticity back to the dead person and make his limbs move again. This magical ritual is preserved in fascinating hieroglyphics inside the great pyramid of King Unas from the sixth dynasty, located across from the step pyramid of Djoser, in the Saqqara area.

This text suggests a magician-priest who is speaking from the back of the tomb:

Rise up, Pharaoh Unas! Raise your head, give strength to your bones, gather your arms and legs and shake the earth made of your flesh! Receive from us the bread that does not become mouldy and the beer that does not ferment! Rise up, King Unas! Do not continue not living!

Oh all-powerful sun god! Your son arrives to you, welcome him in your arms! Help him with your strength! King Unas is afraid to go forward alone in the darkness where nothing can be seen... Oh my father, my father in the darkness! Make me a place by your side so that I can become a star and shine at your side like a small lantern and accompany you forever!

This king is now commanding the immortal planets and is navigating in his ship to the shores where happiness reigns and the inhabitants of the Country of Light row the oars for him. King Unas does not remain still, he goes from one side of the Sun-God to the other. His dwelling is in heaven; the throne that King Unas left on earth will neither crumble nor fall.

Thanks to these spells, the deceased would reach the Kingdom of the Dead assured of triumph, but it was a given that there he would submit to a trial. This court was presided over by the god of the kingdom of the dead, Osiris, seated on his golden throne and adorned in full regalia. At his left sat Anubis, the god with the head of a jackal, protector of the dead and mummification. At his right was the god Thot, who was always represented as a scribe that recorded good and bad deeds.

Around the gods sat the jury, who were mere spectators. Three groups of accused men were placed before a grand scale in which their sins and good deeds or spells in their favour were weighed. The accused people whose bad deeds outweighed the good were given to a hybrid monster that lived in the west to be devoured. The lucky ones whose good works prevailed went among the gods to a type of garden where it was assumed that they would devote themselves to growing flowers. Those whose good and bad deeds weighed the same were given to another god, and we are not sure what he did with them, although they may have gone to type of purgatory.

The "Book of the Dead", whose tablets were placed inside the sarcophagus, contained a magical formula so that the deceased person would look good appearing before the gods. This papyrus was placed between the mummy's legs. It is assumed that Anubis would lead them before the court, which might be presided over by Osiris, his sister Nephthys and his sister-wife Isis. The deceased person would address them in this way:

"I greet you, great god, possessor of all truths. Having been led into your presence, I have seen your perfection. I know you, I know your name as I do that of the forty-two gods that accompany you in this trial, acting as guardians of the evil, with whose blood they quench their thirst on this day on which the Good Being must assess our works."

Immediately thereafter, the dead person made a long declaration of innocence, always negative, in order to make it clear that he had not committed the sins of which he might be accused. It is interesting to read these:

I have not mistreated my family... I have not made anyone work beyond their capacity... I have not treated the poor harshly... I have not been selfish... I have not cheated on measures of wheat... I have not deceived the measuring of maps... I have not tinkered with the scale's counterweight...

In this way, the accused person denied having committed sins as many as thirty-six times. In order to ensure his pardon, he began his declaration of innocence once again, addressing himself successively to each of the forty-two gods, in whose name he continued denying his sin. And he would add:

I am not afraid of falling under the knife of the judges, not only because I have never offended god or the pharaoh, but also because I have also done what pleases the gods. I have given food to the hungry and drink to the thirsty, I have dressed the naked and lent my ship to whoever needed to cross the river. I belong among those to whom people say "Welcome" whenever they see them.

Despite these formulas, the sinner could still not be sure since he feared that once on the scale's tray, his heart would belie the words he had just uttered. In order to prevent this from happening, there was another invocation in chapter 30 of the same book, in which he would say:

Oh my heart! Do not testify against me, do not contradict me before the judges, and do not let your weight go against me before the master of the scale.

Using spells in this way, the dead person was proclaimed 'maa kheru' ('righteous in word') and became a subject in the kingdom of Osiris. Some privileged men obtained the title of 'maa kheru' in life through their 'distinguished services' provided to the pharaoh and his court.

A colourful story

One of the most colourful stories from Egypt comes from the mummy of the mother of the pharaoh Cheops, builder of the Great Pyramid and son of Snefru, founder of the fourth dynasty. When the American University, Harvard, and the Boston Museum delegated the research of the Giza plateau to the archaeologist Reisner, they hoped to find something wonderful in the shadows of the Great Pyramid.

In 1928, they discovered a tiled passageway which covered an underground hiding place under a layer of plaster. After excavating, they found a bricked-in slab behind which lay steps that led to a 82 feet deep well dug into the rock and full of stones.

Once all the material was extracted, they located the entrance to a burial chamber, where there was an alabaster sarcophagus and a profusion of broken furniture, which has now been totally restored in such a way to demonstrate that no one had opened that tomb before and that it had been sealed ever since its construction more than 4,500 years ago. This filled the researcher with great hopes.

They were thus impatient when they raised the sepulchre, because they wished to see the features of the mother of the builder of the Great Pyramid. What a surprise when they opened the sarcophagus only to discover that it was empty... Where was the mummy? Were they facing yet another case of 'walking mummies'? Should they believe those stories that were being published in the most sensationalist newspapers?

Today the mystery has been solved. The queen was buried along with her husband in the celebrated Pyramid of Dashur (the second step pyramid built in Egypt. The first belonged to Djoser, located in Saqqara, and is also stepped. The third pyramid, with smooth sides and the largest of all, is that of Cheops). This pyramid was violated during Cheops' life, as we know, because when he found out he ordered that a much larger and safer pyramid be built.

Thus the Great Pyramid was constructed: 479 feet high and made with 88,286,812 ft^3 of stones. In addition, he ordered that a new tomb be prepared for his mother, since probably no one dared to tell him that the mummy had been destroyed and that furthermore its whereabouts were not known. As you can see, the fantastic funeral of Cheops' mother took place around an empty sarcophagus. Queen Hathepshut died approximately in the year 2,600 BC.

Tutankhamen's curse

The pharaohs' tombs were also protected by magic. The most famous case was the violation of Tutankhamen's tomb and its more or less fantastical consequences, which were reported across the world by the press, giving way to infinite novels and several movies. Indeed, during the 1926 tourist season, about 13,000 persons visited Tutankhamen's tomb; meanwhile, representatives of about three hundred scientific societies toured the laboratory facilities.

The popularity of these discoveries was why a chain of consequences achieved world-wide notoriety, which the tabloid press labelled 'the pharaoh's curse'. It all began with the publication of the fact that magical texts had been found in the royal tomb, containing curses on the king's enemies, centred round four magical figures oriented toward the four cardinal directions in order to release the royal mummy from his enemies, a threat that many kept in mind.

The beginning of the journalistic frenzy came with the death of Lord Carnavon from a mosquito bite on the 6th April, 1923, months after having been the first person to penetrate Tutankhamen's tomb. Everything would have ended there if the people in Europe had not been ignorant about the sanitary conditions in Egypt (and the ferocity of its mosquitoes) and the campaigns organised by the many organisations that so pervade England against the desecration of graves that would have been desecrated anyhow, with less usefulness and respect, by the professional thieves of El Gurnah.

Shortly thereafter, there was another victim to the curse; later came a third, then a fourth. On the 21st February, 1930, the newspapers reported the fourteen and nineteenth victims with these words:

Today Lord Westbury, seventy-eight years old, threw himself from a seventh floor window of his home in London, dying in the act. His son, who participated in the excavation of Tutankhamen's tomb a few years back as the secretary of the researcher, Mr Carter, was found dead in November of last year at his home despite the fact that he had gone to bed in perfect health. The cause of his death has not been determined.

The twenty-first victim was the Egyptologist, Arthur Weigall, *from the effects of an unknown fever.* The twenty-third victim was Archibald Douglas Reid, who died suddenly when examining a mummy using X-rays. Shortly thereafter C. Mace also lost his life, one of the first men to penetrate the burial chamber. Then Lord Carnavon's step-brother, Aubrey Herbert, committed suicide. But the list of coincidences went on. In February, 1929, the wife of the researcher, Elisabeth Carnavon, died from a 'mosquito bite'. In 1930, only the tomb's discoverer, Howard Carter, remained alive.

There were infinite theories attempting to explain this series of deaths, which were difficult to attribute to mere coincidence. One of these theories was examined by a doctor from the hospital in Port Elizabeth, Republic of South Africa, Doctor Geoffrey Dean, who had discovered in one of his patients the same symptoms of disease that affected various Egyptologists, although it could not be extended to cover all of those who had died as a result of 'Tutankhamen's curse'. This disease was none other than histoplasmosis, or the 'cave disease', which is spread by poisonous microscopic fungi that grow in darkness, among dust and organic detritus. The disease is quite common among people that have spent much time underground, especially in places with bats.

The effects of radiation

Another fascinating theory is related to the use of radioactive materials in mummification, to which we referred earlier. We must inevitably accept the fact that the ancient Egyptians had some system of illumination that allowed them to devote a great deal of time to painting and relief carving inside the tombs without using either torches or any other system that would have left smoke on the ceiling. We should bear in mind that the tombs in the Valley of the Kings, which were worked and painted in situ and excavated in bare rock, did not present even the slightest trace of smoke.

This mystery has been explained by various specialists as the result of the application of an ingenious system of mirrors, which those who have personally seen the Valley of the Kings cannot accept. The other theory, defended by Egyptian guides and some of the country's best researchers, states that the ancient Egyptians knew about and made use of the properties of certain radioactive substances, which are found in their natural state on the shores of the Red Sea, in order to have a source of cold light (a material similar to phosphorus).

If we accept that a radioactive source might have been used, we can explain the similarity between the clinical histories of the deceased expeditionary members 'as a result of insect bites' and the hair-raising symptoms found in the Atomic Hospital in Hiroshima among those affected by the terrible 1945 atomic explosion, which even altered the physiological characteristics of their descendants.

The issue of 'Tutankhamen's curse' has never ceased to fascinate the general public, since so many deaths and coincidences remain a mystery. Modern human beings refuse to accept the intervention of supernatural powers and attempt to explain the deeds, even the most incomprehensible of them, using reason and science. Nevertheless, when we are faced with the hieratic, faraway and at the same time poetic and mysterious world that is ancient Egypt, we cannot help think that a superhuman explanation of the enigmas might be the right one.

Chapter V

THE ENIGMA OF THE SPHINXES

Flaubert's enthusiastic point of view

On the 7th December, 1849, the French novelist Gustave Flaubert, author of such brilliants works as "Madame Bovary" and "Salambo", wrote of this experience with a sphinx:

It was not yet three p.m. when we began to see the first signs of the desert where the three pyramids had been built. I was so eager to see them, to stand in front of them, that I started to gallop my horse over the sands. I was soon jointed by Maxim. Both of us proceeded on a crazy ride.

Soon we found ourselves before the sphinx of Abu-el-Hol (called the father of terror), which is what he is called by the Arabs. I was surprised by the predominance of grey as far as the eye could see, since both the sand and the pyramids were this colour. But to me it seemed beautiful, perhaps because it was bathed in an increasingly pinkish light which contrasted with the intense blue of the sky. Suddenly, a flock of eagles began to fly quite slowly about the summits of the great monuments. We had to stop before the sphinx, impressed by the intensity of its look, as if it were threatening us. I could see that Maxim had become pale. But I was not impassive, since I felt as if my head was victim to a kind of whirlwind. I made a futile attempt to control my emotions.

I looked once again at the sphinx. Its eyes continued to be filled with great expressiveness, with a life that made me uneasy. Some birds had just perched precisely in the left eye, although this did not prevent me from seeing that it was an unsettling white. The entire complex looked toward the east, which resulted in the emphasis of the grey of the enormous head and the colossal separated ears, similar to those of Negroes. I imagine that this thin neck must have weathered the tempests of the desert sand...

It is easy to tell that this commentary does not come from a bored person, or from one who wishes to return to his homeland, France, something Flaubert had been clamouring for almost since the moment he had embarked for Egypt. He continued the journey because he had promised to do so; in addition, he needed to recover from the failure of his latest work. Nevertheless, as soon as he drew near the pyramids his mood changed, as if the fabulous ruins had bewitched him.

Something else happened to him. After seeing the sphinx of Abu-el-Hol, he had a moment of inspiration, which led him to utter these words: *Bovary...! Madame Bovary! I've got it!* Is it possible that his experience with the sphinx helped him to begin his greatest novel, even though it had nothing to do with Egypt?

The sphinxes were men

Nowadays, one does not need to ride a horse to visit the sphinxes, unless one wishes to ride camels on a tourist's whim. Motorways have been built for cars and other vehicles, kept at a safe distance. But one could say that the desert sand is the same. Another modern-day advantage is that the sphinxes are seen 'barer'; that is, they are not covered with sand as in Flaubert's time.

Egyptian sphinxes are quite different from Greek ones, since a man's head, generally that of a pharaoh, is placed on top of a lion's body. The Hellenic sphinxes show the body of a lion and a woman's head. The historian Hans Gerhard Evers wrote about this matter:

The evidence that a large number of the Egyptian sphinxes represented kings or pharaohs and not princesses stoked great disbelief, in addition to bitter controversy. When the situation calmed down a bit, the innovators began to write the sphinx in foreign languages using the masculine gender in order to adapt to the change, without taking the custom into account. Fortunately it was a passing fashion since it sounded so bad. It is logical that we return to what is traditional. Would it occur to someone to use the masculine gender for statue in instead of the correct feminine gender simply because the person sculpted was a man the likes of Napoleon or Apollo? Likewise, the sphinx is a general word defining a symbolic representation of man and beast. Whoever is dissatisfied with my explanation and thinks that the word is most properly and accurately written according to the sex of the person will come upon serious obstacles on many occasions since in Egypt one can find sphinxes with women's and rams' heads, in addition to those representing kings and pharaohs...

Besides the semantic question, it is important to emphasize that few visitors have not been impressed by the sphinxes, especially the one at Giza.

The sphinxes suggest great mysteries

Little is known about the origin of the sphinxes, although it is clear that they date from before the pyramids. Some historians, such as Dimitri Merejkowski, have demonstrated that the sphinxes are the most ancient statues of the human face known to humankind.

What there is no doubt about is that they join human beings and beasts, with the beast at rest while the man or woman's head is extremely majestic and impressive. The first sculptor who dared to create a sphinx must have had the intention of frightening people – and he succeeded!

Because the rational and the irrational, human and beastly strength, the greatness of different yet perfectly complementary royalties are captured in this figure, as are so many other things... Perhaps because we mere mortals are given to the most frightening fantasies, many of those who see an Egyptian sphinx for the first time feel frightened.

But seeing it in a museum is not the same as in a desert, with the play of light and shadows, with the cloying heat, with the sense of antiquity... Knowing that you have before you a monument that was sculpted almost 40 centuries ago!

No one has been able to destroy their beauty

The damage that the great heads of the sphinxes have suffered is due more to the action of human barbarism than to the passage of time. We have enough information to know that the most brutal mutilations took place during the period of Arab domination. For example, the Mameluks tested their aim with firearms by using these gigantic works of art as their targets.

The greatest destruction visible on their heads and some parts of the body was caused by cannon balls. None of them were launched during wartime, rather at the whim of some irresponsible person who decided to use these parts of the sphinxes as their targets.

It is certain that as it lifts the desert sand, the wind has unwittingly acted like a fanciful plane, since its irregular effects can be seen in many different places. There is no doubt that nothing and no one has been able to damage the sphinxes' beauty, their distinction. They remain there, just as they were 4,000 years ago, looking toward infinity, more impressive than a mountain or any other natural monument because they are the testimony of a civilisation that knew the art of the transcendental, of immortality.

It is worth recalling, at this point, what Kurt Lange wrote in his book "Pyramiden, Sphinxe, Pharaonen":

The enormous lion, whose head is covered by the trapezoidal headdress of the pharaohs, rises in the centre of a broad quarry to the east of the Pyramid of Khafre, next to a road that leads from the hollow of the sphinx to the funeral temple of this king, located in front of the pyramid. So, nowadays, one can see the entire complex from head to foot, from the edges of the hollow. During the long process of its cre-

66

ation, we are sure that the stonemasons faced a barrier of limestone rock in a yellowish-grey tone, which was softer than the rest, and whose poor resistance prevented it from being used in the ashlars of the pyramids. It is possible that they halted work to consult their supervisors, who would have ended up asking Khafre's opinion. And after listening to his architects' advice, he would have been the one to decide that this different limestone rock be used to sculpt a sphinx of immense, monumental proportions.

Whether tradition tells us the truth or a falsehood is, in this case, irrelevant. It is important to realize that this enterprise came from the creative, titanic and yet ingenuous will of a civilisation that had still not reached maturity...

Historians have not agreed on whether to attribute the great sphinx to Khafre or the pharaoh Tuthmosis IV. What seems to support the former is that it is located in the royal cemetery of the fourth dynasty, while it also somewhat resembles certain statues of Khafre that have been found.

An epic poem

Since they were warriors and adventurers, the majority of the pharaohs from the eighteenth dynasty liked to organise parades under the gaze of the great sphinx. They also chose its base as the starting point for journeys, hunting expeditions or the beginning of battles. Precisely at one of these dazzling sites is where Amenophis II, the tenacious son of the impressive Tuthmosis II, promised to construct a stela on that very site, which he accomplished as soon as he was named sovereign of Egypt.

In excavations carried out approximately thirty years ago near the hollow of the great sphinx, the personal objects of a crown prince were discovered, whose reign must have been quite short. An Egyptian poem was also found, to the joy of the Egyptologists, devoted to this young 18-year-old king. Below is a copy of it as transcribed by S. Schott:

"He navigated on the prow of a vessel with two hundred men.

Everyone rowed strenuously
But after travelling half a mile
They felt their muscles become weak.
They did not have the air they needed...
Thus the king did not hesitate to take the twenty-foot long
oar
And begin rowing strenuously until reaching solid ground
After having rowed about three miles
Without letting go of the oar at any time.
Thus the faces of those who had seen him shone with admiration
Since they were witnesses of such a great feat.
He only tested three hundred great bows
To find out the skill of the builders
And find out who knew his trade and who did not.
I shall narrate his wonders.
He entered into his arms field,
Where four targets of Asian copper had been prepared for him
Each one as thick as a palm,
And twenty feet separated one from the other.
A moment later his majesty appeared in his chariot
Just like the god of war with all his might.
He prepared his bow
And four arrows at the same time.
He looked at what was before him and shot,
With the splendour of the god of war.
All the arrows hit the targets
And were driven into the closest post.
This was something never before seen, unheard of.
Not even in the legends had it ever happened
That arrows shot against a copper target
Went through it and knocked it to the ground...

In this epic poem, we witness the deed of an archer who is able to shoot four arrows at the same time at the same number of shields, something that only a demigod, a divine hero, could do. The ending also reveals that at this time a metal had been discovered even that was more resistant than copper, which must have been iron, the same metal that would later be found in the excavations of the Great Pyramid of Cheops to everyone's surprise, since it was not believed that the Egyptians had such a precious metal at their disposal.

Let us continue with the legend

Tuthmosis IV was one of the first pharaohs to make sure that the sphinxes and pyramids were not covered by the desert sands. Precisely one of these disinterments took place along with the restoration of the Great Sphinx. The result must have been so highly appreciated by everybody that it deserved the honour of being commemorated in a stele. A copy of it is inscribed in the temple of Osiris, and it was later placed between the forelegs of the sphinx, where it remained for many centuries.

Thanks to this inscription we know that the sphinx was considered the representation of the sun god of Heliopolis, Horakhty (*the Horus of the two places where light is born*), and that it was highly venerated by the Egyptian people. This text has also enabled us to learn about an interesting legend.

It appears that the young prince Tuthmosis liked to go hunting in the Memphis desert, almost always in a chariot pulled by magnificent horses *that galloped quicker than the wind*. He used to take his first shot with his bow and arrow at a lion or a gazelle, which he always took down in a race.

One day he felt very tired, and since the hunting had been longer and harder than on other occasions, he sat down at the base of the sphinx. It was during the hottest hours in the afternoon, thus the great god's shade was good for him. Soon after he lay down, he fell asleep. Suddenly, this very god in all his divinity appeared to speak to him with the same tone a father would use with his most beloved son:

Raise your eyes and look at me, oh Tuthmosis! I am your father, the god Horakhty-Kepri-Re-Atum! I shall give you my kingdom. You shall soon ascend to the throne and wear the white and red crown on your head, because you shall occupy the place of Geb, the monarch of the gods. The earth in all its greatness, which shines under the look of the Lord-of-Every-

thing that lives, shall belong to you. The earth, with its immense size, shall be yours, as will the territories that can be reached by the look of fire by he who dominates existence. The treasures of Egypt and its incommensurate tributes paid by other countries shall fill your arks. I have been watching what you do for a long time, because you engage my eyes and my heart. Do you realize how the desert sand that now surrounds me presses on my body? Promise me that you will hear my pleas, since you are my son and my rescuer, and I will never abandon you.

As soon as the prince opened his eyes he knew that this had not been a dream, since the divine voice continued to resonate in his ears. Soon he saw that the promises were true, since he was crowned as the new king of Egypt. He shortly thereafter paid the 'price' stipulated with the god and freed the sphinx from the enormous amount of sand that had imprisoned it.

The true appearance of the Great Sphinx

The Great Sphinx of Giza had noble, harmonious features, wore a snake's head on his forehead and had an impressive beard. He also had a nose, which is now destroyed, as well as a full head and lips. Many of these remains are found in the Museum of Antiquities in Cairo and the British Museum in London.

After the destruction caused by human barbarism, to which we should add that caused by the passage of time and the desert sands, it is important to emphasize the fact that the sphinx has been cared for with obvious affection. In reality, it is one of the elements, if not the most important, used to attract tourism. The fact that its nose is missing has inspired many tales, but it is something that society has accepted, just as the Venus de Milo statue is lacking its arms. This is a reality that offers a glimpse of how something beautiful would be sublime if it were complete.

Let us once again examine the texts of the well-documented Kurt Lange in order to broaden our examination of this topic:

70

The Old Empire has only bequeathed us ruins and pieces of other sphinxes whose minuscule proportions allowed them to be transported to other places in accordance with the requirements of the ceremonies. However, all the sovereigns from the Middle Empire wished to be immortalised through splendid sphinxes made of hard stone. We have to acknowledge that this was the classical period of this type of sculpture; hence, the magnificent artists of the court workshops gave their utmost to creating brilliant works.

The sustained nobility of the seated lion becomes gradually even greater as if the spectator expected the ferocious beast to leap out at any moment. With its solid presence, just as if it were enlarged by a primordial, eternal force, we could say that the calmness of the prodigious figure could only have been achieved through the permanent tension of the members of a body that is ennobled by the existence of the human head, framed by the impressive classical hairstyle, on which the royal headdress appears...

...In the times of the Middle Empire, as a royal statue the sphinx embodied the strength and continuity of the State, which Thebes' perseverance had managed to recover after the fall of the Old Empire, overcoming a century of extremely violent social crisis. We should see this impressive figure as a symbol that has no relationship to the funerary buildings; thus it was raised before the people as a confirmation of the social order and power of the pharaohs...

When the mysteries start to build up

The most daring pyramidologists in their theories, those who are not afraid of reality because they are convinced that there might only be a mask or a decoration hiding the great mysteries, have accepted the idea that the Great Sphinx of Giza, just like the Pyramid of Cheops, lies over a telluric land, that is, over magnetic fields that generate invisible forces, thanks to which a continuous union with the cosmic energies of the solar system is sustained.

One of these audacious men is Ivan Sanderson, an American researcher who is tradition's arch-rival. With a mind free from prejudices, he claimed after carrying out infinite verifi-cations throughout the entire world that on our planet there are twelve centres of points of electromagnetic aberrations, which he has been able to locate on Easter Island, the Devil's Sea, Bermuda, and especially in Egypt, in addition to other places.

Based on this theory, it is impossible to accept the idea that some architects or magician-priests who chose the site where the sphinxes and pyramids were to be located only did so because of the solidity of the land. They must all have known about its electromagnetic properties. However, since they did not act as clairvoyants, they must have learned about it from superior beings, who might have come from outer space or been the sons of extra-terrestrials. They must have adapted to conditions on the Earth, and were not only mortal but also convinced that their science could only be known by a caste of initiates.

Another theory only bandied about among the most risk-taking, is that the sphinxes and pyramids fulfilled much more than just a function as funeral monuments. There might have existed such intense communication between the living, only a few privileged ones, and the dead, that some of them pro-vided this great knowledge. One bit of knowledge could be the existence of this telluric land or electromagnetic subsoil, an idea that is supported by Edgar Cayce when he says that the Egyptian funeral temples acted as intermediaries between the magician-priests and the 'beyond'. Manly P. Hall also claimed that the sphinxes and pyramids were the symbols of the alliance between human beings and External Wisdom. To put it more simply: there existed a direct medium of dialogue between certain men and the gods and goddesses themselves.

But how did this dialogue take place? Was it perhaps men-tal or direct? Might it have taken the form of a sudden or slow inspiration in which the beneficiaries acquired extraor-dinary knowledge that they could not have even imagined before?

Due to the means they must have used to attain this knowl-edge, all of these initiates understood that they had to behave like 'humans'. Thus they created a colossal work involving the entire Egyptian nation, but only they knew that in the

72

monuments secret energy, knowledge and magic would gather which would only be within the reach of those who knew how to decipher them after complicated research.

Another of the great enigmas coming from the sphinxes, just like from the pyramids, is related to what we call the 'beyond'. Our intention is not to paint a 'place' like certain religions tell us to do when talking about a heaven and a hell. Rather we are discussing another unknown dimension, perhaps a universe made up of anti-material, the opposite of everything we know.

The term 'giant' was more than just a word

It is assumed that the giants were born somewhere in Asia, for them to have left footprints of their journey in India and China. But the place where they truly fulfilled their mission is Egypt since the climate, the fertility of the soil and the hospitality of the people invited them to remain there.

These giants could also have been the inhabitants of Atlantis, the majority of whom perished due to the grand cataclysms that shook the world. Nevertheless, some survivors might have reached Egypt, the ideal site for spreading their knowledge through colossal constructions, in which they could enclose a great deal of religiosity.

There is no one better than Max Toth to reason through the theory of this type of religiosity:

On a metaphysical plane, there are two groups within humanity: the wisest souls, who have progressed through their experiences, and the young and neophyte souls. Within the superior group there are those who are willing to take on enough responsibility, enabling them to support the neophyte step in its evolution through a process of initiation. We can say that those masters start from a principle of 'noblesse oblige'. We mean that their position requires them to behave as a type of 'guardian angel', those who take care to maintain existence and at the same time ensure the continuity of everything until eternity. In other words: were the masters to abandon this important mission, life on earth would evaporate and as a result, their own existence would end.

73

Within this spiritual idea is contained the maximum prophecy revealed to us through the pyramid. We should bear in mind that the triangle makes up the totality of the pyramid, just as it gives form to the triple life of the human being. The figure made up of the neophyte in one corner, the master in the other and god in the third, demonstrates the basic principles of the religions. The neophyte can only reach his master's levels when he is most open to establishing perfect communication with God...

We shall also use Max Toth's ideas to continue emphasizing the idea of the 'initiates' as the true creators of the sphinxes and pyramids, a subject that will come up again and again in the following chapters of our book.

Chapter VI

THE GREAT PYRAMID OF CHEOPS

The most ancient conjectures

Nothing is known about how the pyramids were built. We can only glimpse the actual reality through certain shrewd studies that often contradict each other. If we begin by evaluating the conjectures made by the ancient Hebrews, we would have to believe the fact that the pyramids were built to commemorate a great tragedy, perhaps a cataclysm that radically changed the course of history. The cataclysm took place in a planetary system near the Earth, and it unleashed great floods and dreadful fires.

Another of the conjectures by the ancient Arabs tells us that the pyramids were erected long before the universal flood, after a king had a vision in which the world was shown totally upside down and the stars were falling from the sky. But this visionary monarch did not content himself with only building such great constructions. He also took pains to see that all the knowledge that wise men had communicated to him, covering such diverse fields as geometry, astronomy, physics, working with precious stones, the best system for manufacturing mysterious machines, as well as malleable crystals and many other things unknown in this age were inscribed in the form of hieroglyphics inside them.

The ancient Hebrews' conjecture refers to the fact that the Scythian people possessed such great knowledge about the movement of the planets and other celestial bodies that they built two pyramids, one of stone and the other of brick, in order to enclose their science within them.

The mystery of the Great Pyramid

In his book "The mystery of the Great Pyramid", the theosophist Basil Steward claimed that its builders could only have been the Egyptians. Nevertheless, without the help of colonisers from Asia who possessed fabulous scientific and mathematical knowledge, they would never have accomplished it. *These privileged beings belonged to the white civilisation of the Adamites, bearer of uncommon moral and religious principles that allowed them to attain scientific and cultural achievements that were very advanced compared to the other civilisations of their time.*

Other Egyptologists agree with this idea, since they believe that the perfection seen in the initial period of Egyptian architecture can only be explained by the idea of a group of artists and wise men, masters in infinite disciplines and with portentous skill much greater than that of their counterparts. With regards to the Great Pyramid, Petrie believed that *"it is the work of a single man, of a genius capable of carrying out the most prodigious labour and then disappearing without leaving a trace."*

What were the Soviets able to discover?

In his book "Timeless Earth" published in 1969, Peter Kolosimo claimed that the Soviets discovered in Egypt a multitude of wondrous objects related to archaeology: astronomic maps describing the position of the stars millions of years ago and high precision spherical crystal lenses which might have been used for telescopes and other devices.

The Soviets not only found a multitude of extraordinary objects, their studies also enabled them to reach the conclusion that *the Egyptians came from Indonesia, whence they were forced to flee approximately twelve thousand years ago due to a catastrophe of cosmic origin, since the impact of a giant meteor had destroyed almost their entire country.*

The first steps in its construction

In many of the most important matters related to Egypt, one must start from theories, since the hieroglyphics found in the tombs are not very explicit on this point. Thanks to evidence from R. L. Engelbach, we know that the sand and gravel were usually dug away in order to reach bare rock. Then this rock was worked in order to eliminate the depressions and cut away all the bumps.

In order to have more secure foundations, the four sides of the base were usually surrounded by mud from the Nile and then filled with water, forming a reticule of equal squares. The work was so precise that there was not even an inch of slope. Then, a row of rectangular white limestone rocks was put into place to serve as the foundation for the stones that would cover the pyramid.

The most wonderful work is evident in the fact that when they carried out the exact calculation of the first straight side of a pyramid, these brilliant architects took as their reference point the dawning and setting of the circumpolar stars, some of which could be seen in the alpha of the Dragon. Later, they devoted themselves to setting and placing in bare rock the enormous limestone ashlars. This allowed them to form the cardinal angles on which they would place the first rows of the outside rock.

A great many of the limestone blocks were extracted from the Mokattam quarries just a few miles from the Arabic shore of the Nile. Others were taken from a place near the Giza plateau. One of the unique characteristics of these works can be observed in the way the stonemasons painted the blocks that they worked with their seal, perhaps in order to bear witness to their work. This is why they wrote: 'Jump Gang' or 'Vigorous Gang'.

The great granite blocks

It is assumed that the great granite blocks weighing seventy tonnes with which the Chamber of the King in the Great Pyramid was built were taken from the Aswan quarries, very close to Siena, a place that was some three hundred and eighty miles up the Nile. They were later transported on large barges.

The stonemasons from the first dynasty had copper tools such as saws and chisels which they used to cut the limestone or drill and polish the granite with a skill that today seems marvellous to us. It is assumed that they sanded such hard material using dampened quartz grains with an abrasive product.

Vestiges of the master stonemasons' labour have been found in what used to be the Mokattam quarries. And so we know that they dug into the several hundred-feet long hard rock tunnels. They then sectioned off spaces between the blocks and the ceiling in order to be able to loosen them. To do this, they used wooden maces and copper chisels which had been given an extraordinary temper (using forging techniques that we have not yet discovered). In this way they managed to open a large crack in the rock wall into which they placed wedges made of moistened wood. Thus the block came loose without any of its edges being damaged. On occasions they exchanged the wedges for hot water, which they poured onto the crack, since in this way the rock cut was flawless.

The human dragging of the great blocks

Herodotus wrote that twenty years and participation by hundreds of thousands of workers, who were relieved by an equal number every three months, were needed in order to build the Great Pyramids. In order to transport the huge granite blocks, a huge roadway about 2,952 feet long and 59 feet wide was cleared. It took ten years to finish it. All of this was certainly made of polished stone, thus allowing the huge blocks to be slid from the Nile to the Giza plateau.

At the end of the past century, the distinguished American naval attaché in Egypt, F. M. Barber, wrote a small work entitled "Mechanical Triumphs of the Ancient Egyptians". Since he had been able to make his own observations of the land itself, he deduced that the roadway used to transport the gigantic rocks must have had a slope of 118 feet above the Nile. This was the only possible way of managing to transport these rocks on a surface that, in addition to being polished, must have been very well lubricated.

With regard to the men who moved the blocks, he calculated that there may have been eight hundred of them well tied and in a double row, pulling four thick ropes. With proper alignment, working all at the same time in rhythm with a chant or cries from the mouth of the time-keeper, they would be strong enough.

This is something that has never been accomplished using animals; even the strongest well-trained oxen could never achieve perfect synchronisation like human beings. Let us imagine what happens in a tug of war, in which the two groups pull in the opposite direction in order to pull the other team over the dividing line. The group that best coordinates its efforts always wins, because if they apply themselves at the same time they can overcome another person who individually would be stronger. But the Egyptian pullers must have made a staggered effort which could not have lasted more than a few hours. After this time, the first group of eight hundred pullers was relieved.

The construction of the Great Pyramid

Few Egyptologists agree on how the Great Pyramid was built. To Herodotus, the most ancient among them, they were begun from the top. Once the apex was completed, the successive rows were made from the top down. To do so they needed four ramps and a series of wood machines which helped to move the huge blocks, an enterprise that many consider impossible since only human effort and elementary tools were used, since it took one month just to move one block.

Although only twenty-five percent agree with it, the most widely supported idea is that construction began with the base and then continued upward, row by row. Using this method, more than five hundred granite blocks could be put into place every day. Nevertheless, given the fact that all of the base rows have more than fifty thousand blocks, it would have taken more than three months just to build a single row... Should we perhaps assume that a superior power that had little to do with the simple use of human physical force or more or less effective devices intervened in this entire process? Should we continue to consider the extra-terrestrials?

If human beings had built it

It has been calculated that the Great Pyramid is made up of about 2,300,000 blocks weighing 2.5 tonnes each. The average dimensions of each block are 3.9 x 3.9 x 2.3 feet. If eight workers were capable of transporting ten blocks in three months, 100,000 workers would have been capable of moving 125,000 in the same amount of time. This would cover the twenty years that Herodotus said had been needed to build the Great Pyramid.

It is obvious that not only pullers, ramp workers and architects participated in this enormous job, since it has been calculated that a similar number of men worked in the quarries, the barges that sailed on the Nile and the different gathering points for the rocks.

If to all this we add the artists who built the interior of the Pyramid, with their labyrinths, halls, figures and inscriptions and ornaments, we have no choice but to accept the idea that all of Egypt was involved in the construction of the pyramids.

The idea that the huge blocks fit perfectly on top of each other without having to use any kind of mortar has been refuted by the Italian researchers, Maragioglio and Rinaldi in their book "The Architecture of the Memphis Pyramids". Both were able to prove that a fine layer of very fluid mortar was used, which acted as a lubricant and filler. It is possible that this disappeared with the passage of time and the intense heat, after performing its role, and thus it has been so difficult to discover its existence.

The enormous efforts of the auxiliary workers

One of the issues that most astounds Egyptologists is the team supervising the construction's capacity for organising, since they had to oversee the work, the supplies, the hospitals, the dwellings and the army. During the times when slaves were used for these enormous jobs, they needed more than 400,000 soldiers to maintain law and order. This leads us to imagine an immense community, greater than all the inhabitants living in the largest cities of the time, a confluence of professional, social and religious interests that the world has only known since the appearance of the large urban metropolises.

The historian August Mencken has made it clear that the men who worked on the Great Pyramid were neither chaste nor saintly. Along with them there were around 150,000 women and children, given the fact that a great many of the workers were married. With regards to their housing, they simply had small lean-tos due to the high daytime temperatures, which fell considerably at night.

Some questions whether it was a human endeavour

William Kingsland took pains to put a stop to the idea that the pyramids were built in the time specified by Herodotus. For this to have taken place, the 2,300,000 granite blocks would have needed 7,300 days of work, which would have meant placing 315 blocks per day, that is, 26 per hour during twelve hours of work per day. Should we perhaps think that they worked all night long because they had some type of illumination?

The Egyptians did not have such knowledge because it is known that they rested at night. Kingsland also questions the illumination used by the architects, workers and artists who worked inside the Great Pyramid. To this he adds the means used for enough air to reach the extremely large and intricate galleries. His conclusion is that they used means that we do not know about today; thus, he considers them 'occult'.

Various possibilities worth examining

When cutting the huge granite blocks in the quarries, the question that remains inexplicable for the majority of Egyptologists is the following: *how did they cut the bottom side, the part that was inaccessible since it was inside?* It is assumed that the quarries had marvellous mechanical devices that could be inserted by the cuts already made from the outside with sheets more than a metre (3 feet) long that had to begin to cut when their tip, which must also have measured a metre (3 feet), was folded in order to begin the blind cut. This seems hard to believe. It is clear that if the Egyptians had had some type of laser, similar to what is currently used to make 'clean cuts' in the hardest and most delicate materials, such as human tissue, they would have got the results that are now being questioned.

They might also have had other more effective means than the laser. If we set out to solve the mystery, nothing stops us from using our imagination in all its capacity.

Von Däniken did just that when he demonstrated that the Egyptians were helped by extraterrestrial beings. So, they were able to move the huge stone blocks as if they were virtually weightless, since they had 'anti-gravity' means which cancelled out weight. Jacques Bergier and Louis Pauwels also showed us that certain leaps by humanity, such as the use of metal, could have reached human beings through creatures who came from outer space.

These 'fantastical' theories which dare to explain the great mysteries of the Great Pyramid, have the valuable support of a very ancient Arab legend. It refers to an extraordinary sheet of paper, on which certain sacred words had been written. The sheet was attached to a heavy, voluminous granite block on which certain magical drawings had been engraved. After taking a hammer to the whole, without any of its parts being broken, it could be transported by a single person since it had lost so much weight that it was as light as a feather.

Max Toth says the following about these matters:

The majority of the superstitions and fairy tales in the world contain a grain of truth, which acts as the basis for their plot. This leads us to believe that in all of them there exists a part of reality.

This possibility is easy to demonstrate if we look at the advanced electronic technology from our age, which provides industry with micro-miniature circuits with multiple applications. We thus have manual electronic calculators and other devices which have been used by different space agencies, such as NASA. If we examine their circuits under a microscope, they resemble road maps or even minuscule hieroglyphic inscriptions, facts that arouse our imaginations.

I would say that it could be, due to a faulty translation of the ancient texts, which after having been in contact with the stone block left it as light as a feather, that the Arab legend of the holy paper refers to a circuit imprinted on a thickness of a 0.03 in. The 'hammer' could have been a battery or a cell of electronic energy, which when it made contact with (instead of 'hitting') certain places on the electronic device, managed to activate it such that it enabled it to overcome the effects of gravity. This would allow the stone to float, so not only could it be moved by pulling, it would also be quite easy to lift.

As we can see, the explanations for the mysteries are as numerous as can be absorbed by an open mind, and they are supported by past events and then compared with the achievements of the present. This allows us to keep thinking that when we learn fragments of the truth it is valid to attempt to explain them, without prejudices, using them in an intelligent way.

Another interesting theory

One of the most interesting aspects of the work of the stonemasons is their use of drills. The use of these devices was studied by Petrie after having been advised by different

83

specialists. This led him to claim that not even by using the most modern current technology, even lasers, would it have been possible to find a tool of such amazing properties.

We have to uphold this idea, because the most effective drills that can be found on the market today, those used for drilling quartzite or diorite, can only achieve a maximum penetration of 0.001 inches per turn, while the Egyptian drills, as can be seen by the spirals left on the excavated rocks and the wood, managed to penetrate one hundred times deeper.

Chapter VII

THE TEMPLE OF THE GODS

The mysteries of initiation

There are many Egyptologists who share the idea that the Great Pyramid was constructed by 'initiates', or lesser gods, in order to make it the greatest library for knowledge that could only be interpreted by other 'initiates'. Basically, this knowledge consisted in the great principles and laws of the cosmos and their relationship with human beings.

As has happened since the beginning of religions, *great wisdom distances itself from the ignorant, since it is incapable of elevating itself above the level of crude realism, interpreting things simply by their appearances.*

The modern Masons view the 'Egyptian Order of the Temple' as a series of degrees of initiation, to which anyone wishing to enter must submit. Thus they believe that the Great Pyramid of Cheops is the highest degree since in the country of the pharaohs the 'initiates' were subjected to a twenty-two year long learning process for them to learn all the sciences of the world, especially geometry and mathematics.

Thus, in his book "The Secrets of Ancient Geometry", Tons Brunes writes: *It should not surprise us that the Egyptian priests had included this science in the structure of the temple of initiation since they considered it one of the foundations of divinity.*

Astronomy was also considered essential knowledge, especially because it was linked to astrology, since this was *a profoundly esoteric science that was related to the great cycles in human evolution, which could only be known by the members of a caste of wise men.*

In her book "The Secret Doctrine", the theosophist, H. P. Blavatasky, claims *that in addition to marking the orbits followed by the stars in the firmament, the Pyramid constituted the indestructible symbol of the mysteries and initiations on Earth... Inside it men became elevated to the status of gods, and the gods descended to the place occupied by men. But it was in the space in the middle of the Temple where the neophyte was reborn, in a type of baptismal stoup, in order to become an initiate or an adept.*

Before this, the neophyte who wished to become an initiate had to subject himself to different trials. He was tied to a divan in the shape of Tau so that he fell into a deep sleep. He was left thus for three days and three nights. During this period of time his spiritual self managed to dialogue with the gods and descend to the Country of the Dead, where he was allowed to perform charitable works to benefit the invisible beings... One of the places chosen for this ceremony was the Chamber of the King in the Pyramid of Cheops, where at a certain hour the rays of the rising sun would fall on the neophyte's face without awakening him from his lengthy trance. Then it was believed that he was being initiated by the gods Osiris, Thot and the god of Wisdom...

The most famous initiates

Many Egyptologists see the Great Pyramid's Chamber of the King as a temple for initiates, instead of the tomb of the pharaoh Cheops as others believe. To them, the Egyptian monarch was the guardian of part of the divine 'ka' and had been mummified for this reason; he would continue to keep his divinity since his body would not be damaged by the passage of time. This rite had allowed the status of god to be passed on to his son, without him losing it.

In reality, mummification was the best way to give the pharaoh, as well as anyone who benefited from it, a condition of 'latent life'. The pharaoh could never lose his status as god, so, while his body was being embalmed, a statue of him was kept in the Chamber of the Queen, where it was subjected to *the ceremony of opening the eyes and the mouth, in order to prevent it from ever losing its magical existence.*

It is believed that the majority of the greatest philosophers and religious masters were initiated in Egypt, among them Moses and Saint Paul, as well as Sophocles, Plato, Cicero, Salon, Heraclitus, Pindar, Pythagoras, etc.

The secret geometry

Various Egyptologists, including J. Ralston Skinner and Tons Brunes, have shown that the pyramids are linked to the Jewish Cabbala. As we know, this book tells the key secrets of the Bible, some of which 'hide' the basic roots, all of them cosmic, of the origin of human beings. They go further in their theories, since the Cabbala also must be seen in geometric relation to the area of a circle inscribed in a square, or a sphere in a cube. This enables us to reach the relationship existing between diameter and circumference, whose numerical value can be expressed in integers, such as 22/7. This has always been considered supreme and is associated with the names of the gods Elohim and Jehovah, since the first can be compared to the circumference while the second resembles the diameter.

...Nevertheless, the pyramids were designed based on a highly advanced, totally secret geometry which is only known by the initiates, some of whose fragments might have been incorporated into the works of the Greeks and the classical Alexandrians...

Brunes demonstrated that the ancient Egyptians used the essential design of a circle inscribed in a square to geometrically divide the two figures in equal parts from two to ten, as well as all their possible multiples. This made it unnecessary for them to have to take measurements or make arithmetical calculations. They only used a ruler and a compass, two symbols that have been found along with the pyramids in the ancient Masonic orders and which continue to be used today.

In this 'secret' or divine geometry, the Egyptian initiates also used the cross, since when uniting it with the circle and the square they found the solution to all geometric problems, and it also gave shape to the keys of the numbers and the alphabet. In order to achieve the latter, they only needed to use diagonal lines.

Within their ingenious theories, Tons Brunes believed that geometry was the principle of all sciences, since they did not come from mathematics or the alphabet, so it had to be considered the mother of the numbers and letters. He took as his basis the fact that the ancient Egyptians believed that that circle, the square, the cross and the triangle were divine signs, thus applying them so profusely in the pyramids.

With the simple fact of using a circle inscribed in a square, which was also divided into fourths with a cross, they could compose the basic geometric figures: pentagon, hexagon, octagon and decagon.

The Egyptian initiates were familiar with the metre

In his geometric theories, Brunes includes his certainty that Moses was an Egyptian initiate, or a lesser god, and he thus transmitted his knowledge to the Hebrew architects who built the Tabernacle. This knowledge ended up being included in the sacred teachings.

Great mathematicians who are fascinated by archaeology, such as the Frenchman Charles Funk-Hellet, have demonstrated that the cubit, a basic measurement of the Egyptians and the Hebrews, equalled $pi/6$, which is 26.61 inches. When Solomon ordered the architect Hiram Abiff to build the Temple, he recommended that the columns be 18 cubits high and 12 cubits in circumference at their highest point. In other words, one cubit equalled one-twelfth of the circumference of a 30° arc, which is $pi/6$.

If the circumference was subtracted from the height, the result of 6 linear feet was obtained, which was equal to half of the circumference or the exact value of pi. This surprisingly reveals to us that thousands of years before the birth of Christ, the Hebrews knew that a cubit had a mathematical value that depended on the circumference. This allowed them to resolve *pi* up to the ten-thousandth degree.

They then used a unit of measure such as the radius of a circle, since the Egyptians and Hebrews knew that the trigonometric value of 30° was *pi*/6, that is, the royal cubit, or 0.5236 of the unit used:

$$\frac{3.1416}{6} = 0.5236$$

Funk-Hellet demonstrated that in the year 4,000 BC, the Chaldeans had a mathematical series that provided them with precise values of the cubit, the metre (3 feet) and *pi*. He went even further, since he proved that the metre we use nowadays, developed by the French in the nineteenth century, was already known in antiquity by the Egyptian initiates, since it formed part of their secret knowledge. Precisely the metre was trigonometrically linked to the cubit.

The Great Pyramid appears to be a gnomon or a geodesic pillar, for the construction of which the metre and the cubit were used. Thus in the Chamber of the King, the double square of the floor reaches the measurement of 17.78 feet by 34,356 feet. In reality, the basic unit of the metre formed part of the secret, with the intention that all the calculations could only be done by the initiates or priests. These include the exact duration of the year.

The paintings that covered the pyramids

At the beginning of the nineteenth century, Sir John Herschel attempted to calculate the radius of the Earth. To do so he placed two observers 10,006 feet above sea level. He then made sure that they could no longer see each other when they were 42,234 feet apart, which led him to deduce that the Earth's radius was 4,220 miles. But he erred by 260 miles according to current measurements.

This did not happen to the Egyptian initiates, these gods, since the complete apothem of the Great Pyramid is 10,000 cubits long, which is 6,135 feet. The resulting radius must measure 12,303 feet. The most modern experiments have proven that light completely disappears on the horizon at 12,303 feet, when the observer's eye is located exactly one metre (3 feet) above the ground.

The Argentine Jose Ivarez Lopez tells us, in his work "Physics and Creationism", that in the solar system, all the planets revolve in harmonious orbits which can be measured using a sole unit of length: the metre (3 feet). This was what the Egyptians considered 'natural', since it allowed them to communicate all their mathematical and geometric knowledge.

Colours had also been assigned to each planet: red for Mars, yellow for Jupiter, yellowish green for Saturn, green for Uranus, blue for Neptune and violet for Pluto. They thus painted the pyramids using these colours, placing the red of Mars in the highest places and leaving the base of the pyramids assigned to the sun in yellow. The other colours graded along the walls, representing the solar location according to their position in the sky.

It is true that the pyramids were painted, although today this cannot be seen since all their coverings have disappeared. Nevertheless, some archaeological remains, as well as certain Arab legends, make it clear that this painting existed. In fact, the remains were analysed at the Sorbonne, where it was proven that they formed part of the decoration of a pyramid and, more importantly, that they had been painted using a substance that gave a red ochre colour, while this colour was not considered the natural effect of the chemical deformation of the stones.

Knowledge belonging to gods

The Argentine researcher was also able to demonstrate that the Great Pyramid was the representation of a decimal plan of the solar system. This led him to deduce that the height of the funeral monument must have been one-millionth the distance from the Earth to the Sun, measured from the limits of the atmosphere. He also deduced that the base of the Pyramid represented one-ten thousandth of the surface of the Earth. These data are correct.

Does this knowledge not prove to us that the Egyptian initiates were gods?

Equally amazing, if not more so, is the fact that the box of the Chamber of the King within the Great Pyramid of Cheops has a series of measurements that coincide exactly with infinite astronomic data, which transforms it into an 'atlas of the solar system', because in it we can find the weight of the Earth, the Moon and the Sun with regard to that of the Earth, and an infinite amount of more data. The polar radius of our planet is also included, but measured from one pole to another, always using the metre (3 feet) as the basis.

All this accumulation of data has been obtained from a box that is quite heavily damaged by the passage of time, leading us to imagine the millions of reports it must have compiled when it was built almost 4,000 years ago.

Now that we have touched on its construction, we should mention that the architects of the pyramids, as well as the other elements they contain, must have worked with a watchmaker's precision in order for millions of gigantic granite blocks to compose the most perfect 'astronomical atlas' and at the same time a library in which all the knowledge of the initiates was to be stored, so that it could only be 'read' by other initiates after meticulous observations.

Theories on the height of the Great Pyramid

The marble that covered the primitive Great Pyramid of Cheops might have acted as the 25,000 optical prisms for one of the greatest telescopes, just as at the Palomar Observatory, because each of the marble panels was cut as if it was a mirror. Petrie studied this impressive work, in which he estimated that the precision achieved was similar to that of four flat mirrors which measured about 4.2 acres each.

This is why we should mourn the fact that the marble panels were torn from the Pyramid to be used for lesser purposes, far inferior to their original purpose. It is true that those who committed this barbarous act were not Egyptians, since they had already disappeared as a civilisation, but the dominating Arabs.

We do not wish to put too much blame on these people, because they have passed down to us the texts from the Greek and Roman civilisations, as well as the Persians, Babylonians and other more ancient civilisations, because they did not have the savage custom of ravaging the cultures of their conquered peoples but conserving them in order to take the best from them.

We should perhaps reproach the Egyptian initiates themselves, since by hiding their great knowledge they left only simple monuments for the outsiders: gigantic buildings and figures made of stone that seemed to be 'colossal decorations'. On the other hand, if we bear in mind that the pyramid was linked to geodesic and astronomic structures, we can understand that its height was not just random but precisely a length that in a decimal system represented the distance to the Sun.

Simply by accepting this hypothesis, along with everything discussed before and what we shall explain below, we can understand the effort in precision that the Egyptian architects had to make in order to complete the covering of the pyramid, a work that was addressed to what has been called 'the basic unit of astronomy': the distance separating the Earth from the Sun.

The feat that the sons of the Nile accomplished is supported by two factors: first, the true distance to the Sun; and second, the true height of the pyramid. With regards to the first factor, we must take into account that there are three ways of determining the 'true distance to the Sun'. One of them is related to the shortest distance to the Sun (perihelium); the second is the greatest distance (aphelium); and the third is the average of the greatest radius of the ellipse, which is given the name of 'astronomical unit'.

The most recent astronomic measurements are on the approximation of Eros (made on the 1st January, 1932). The best means were used on this occasion, enabling them to obtain 2,800 photographic plates from twenty astronomical observatories in different countries throughout the world. This made it easier to find out the error caused by atmospheric refraction. After a decade of calculations, it was concluded, in about 1942, that the distance to the sun was 149.679×10^6. Precisely in 1959, Price and Gunn determined the distance to Venus using radar echo. This enabled them to reach the following equation:

$$(149.470 +/- 0.001) \times 106 \text{ km } (1 \text{ mile} = 1,852 \text{ km})$$

Currently, more exact measurements can be obtained using microwaves.

With regards to the true height of the pyramid, the most recent information is 480,954 feet. This calculation assumes that the average value of the four sides of the wonderful architectural complex, the slope of whose sides in turn provide the value of $22/7 = pi$ (Archimedes' essential number).

Different researchers have carried out a series of calculations on the Great Pyramid's height, with errors of less than 0.11 inches on the western side. If we are talking about the entire complex, paying special attention to the measurements taken in the Chamber of the Kings, we can see that the base of the Pyramid is the following:

$$L = (230.355 +/- 0.001) \text{ metres } (1 \text{ foot} = 0,30 \text{ m})$$

Based on this result, it is easy to calculate the height of the pyramid in its relation to the distance to the Sun:

$$R = (146.592 +/- 0.05) \times 10^6 \text{ km}$$

We must accept the potential error in this equation since it contrasts with the small values obtained using radar. This means that we must tolerate a margin of error in the calculations made by the scientists of our age.

This does not affect the Egyptian architects or their astronomers since they proved themselves to be more exact than the astronomers, architects and engineers of the past twenty years. We can say that *all measurements acquire greater meaning when they can be compared, one way or another, with different measurements obtained at different times and in different climatic conditions.*

In accordance with the different measurements obtained during the twentieth century, we can make these valuable comparisons:

Distance to the Sun (perihelium)
(Km x 106)

Year	1900	149.46
Year	1930	149.93
Year	1940	147.97
Year	1960	146.97
Egypt	—-	146.60

Here is the proof that the ancient Egyptians built the Great Pyramid in accordance to the distance to the Sun, something that has been proven based on the references taken from the deteriorated monument. But what would have been obtained by making the calculations from the original Pyramid, with all its impressive covering made of marble panels?

Chapter VIII

THE GREAT PLUNDERERS

The earliest caliphs loved culture

We have already written that the Arabs respected the culture of the people they conquered. Nevertheless, when entering Alexandria, after taking hold of the entire Middle East in the seventh century, they could not find the famous library since it had been plundered long before. But they did find themselves in a magnificent city with four thousand palaces, the same number of baths and almost five hundred theatres.

It is believed that this entire exhibition of art and of refinement changed the purpose of their plundering, so characteristic of the armies of that time. They kept the gold, silver and other metal riches, as well as food and all types of livestock, just as they converted the majority of the inhabitants into slaves.

Nevertheless, the caliphs ordered the conquering troops to take pains to preserve the buildings, gardens and baths. They also commanded them to choose the wisest people in order to teach them how to profit the most from the culture they had discovered. Thus, the dirty Arab from the desert and oasis became a polite, educated person who enjoyed cleanliness and perfumes. The Koran itself, their holy text, promised them the greatest sensual and sexual pleasures in Eden. Why not receive them, albeit on a lesser scale, on Earth itself?

Without forgetting their desire to conquer, the sultans surrounded themselves by translators who knew ancient Greek, Sanskrit and other lost languages. They thus learned about the works of Galen, Euclides, Plato, Aristotle, etc., as well as the great wise men of India. Thanks to this knowledge, the caliphs of Baghdad became the wisest and most powerful. For example, Caliph Harun Al-Rashid paid for each manuscript translated for him its weight in gold; perhaps this is why his feats are celebrated in the book "Arabian Nights".

A prince longing for great knowledge

Harun's son was named Abdullah Al-Mamun. He acceded to the throne in 813. Since he must have been educated by the greatest teachers, his thirst for great knowledge was not selfish or individual, so he made sure that many libraries, several universities, astronomic observatories and theatres were built. His greatest mission was to support the fine arts and all types of culture. He lived in Baghdad, which was known at that time as Dar-al-Salaam, 'the city of peace', where they had fountains that provided more than twelve different types of water, some of which were used to make old men virile or cure different illnesses of the kidneys, digestive tract or circulatory system.

A writer from that age described Al-Mamun as a prince of singular wisdom who attended the assemblies and conferences as an avid listener, although he could have become one of the most educated speakers. We owe to him the first translation of the "Almagest", which is Ptolemy's great treatise on astronomy, in whose pages the most ancient catalogue of the stars known to the world is kept.

Islam's stellar map

One night, Al-Mamun woke up claiming that, in his dreams, Aristotle had appeared to him, ordering him to make an image of the Earth and also to *make a stellar map of Islam*,

96

an enterprise to which he devoted himself with such enthusiasm that within a short time he had hired more than seventy learned researchers. Some of them were in charge of confirming Ptolemy's claim that the Earth's circumference was 18,000 miles.

The first thing these researchers did was to measure the length of a degree of latitude on the plains near the city of Palmira. Since they all moved toward the cardinal points, they quickly reached the conclusion that the latitude had changed a degree. After taking measurements with wooden poles, they obtained a degree of 56 2/3 Arab miles, which equalled 64.39 miles.

Through this figure they reached the conclusion that the circumference of the Earth was 23,315 miles, which perfected Ptolemy's measurements. This figure was impossible to check exactly, since at that time it was believed that the Earth was flat, a notion that the Egyptian astronomers did not share since they knew that the Earth was round, although this secret was enclosed in the Pyramids.

The reports on the measurements of the Earth's circumference, just like the stellar map of Islam and other enterprises by Al-Mamun and his wise associates, were lost in the passage of time. Nevertheless, there are written testimonies as to their existence, since they were examined by the Arab historian Al-Masudi.

The temptation of the Great Pyramid

Al-Mamun must have had something to fear when he used the General Directory of the Post Office as an espionage service, for which about one thousand seven hundred women worked, all of whom took pains to report on 'abnormalities' that took place in Baghdad. Precisely a group of them reached the prince first in order to tell him that there were secret chambers in the Great Pyramid in which maps and tables of the terrestrial sphere were kept.

They also added that there were fabulous treasures and rare objects kept there, such as *weapons that never rust and pieces of crystal that can be bent without breaking*.

97

There is extensive documentation about what happened next. The young caliph did not make haste, even though he was eager for many months. He preferred to take the time to select the best architects, engineers, bricklayers, stonemasons and other artisans. But when he decided to act, he stumbled upon the fact that the Great Pyramid had no door, not even a secret one.

When he asked his 'spies', he found that they had made their report based on legends or stories that were told among certain desert tribes. But he did not punish these women, since he was convinced that the fabulous monument could not be a solid mass of large granite blocks and limestone. He preferred to await the results of the initial work.

This could not have been more disappointing, since the hammers and chisels did not even manage to scratch those hard ashlars. They tried using better tempered tools without accomplishing anything more than chipping the steel. Suddenly, an old blacksmith recalled an ancient system which he carried out without much conviction. This consisted of lighting fires where the granite blocks joined and, when they turned red, soaking them with a large amount of cold vinegar... And the idea worked!

As the large cracks opened, they were able to introduce powerful chisels which gradually made holes. Thus began the first destruction, which would lead to the first pillaging.

Months of tireless work

But the enterprise proved very slow since the stone resisted penetration. Despite the fact that the process used was more or less effective, it forced them to make enormous efforts to proceed just a few feet every day. After two weeks they had only made a very narrow 98 feet tunnel, which was airless and where they had to relieve the stonemasons quite frequently since the smoke from the candles and torches poisoned the air inside.

Given this prospect, Al-Mamun was about to stop work. However, he received that news that one of the workers had just heard some stones falling on the other side of one of the walls in the tunnel that was being dug. Shortly thereafter, the young caliph gave orders to penetrate this wall. And in this way, based on a coincidental event, they found one of the passageways made by the ancient Egyptians!

Specifically, it was a passageway, 3.51 feet wide by 3.9 feet high, which had a steep 26° slope. On the floor, the Arabs found a prismatic stone that had fallen from the ceiling. It was hard for them to remove it. They then had the satisfaction of locating a secret entrance, which was found about 49 feet from the base of the Great Pyramid.

Al-Mamun decided to lead the group of stonemasons. The candles and torches they used for lighting did not poison the air because there was some type of ventilation inside there. The difficult part was going along such slippery slopes where they almost had to go forward on their knees in some places.

After days of exploring this new path they were disappointed to see that there were smoke stains on the ceiling and walls. This led the young caliph to believe that others had been there before him, albeit many years before. Of course they refused to give up. He ordered that they continue the exploration, despite the fact that they came upon numerous obstacles such as blockages that were almost impossible to overcome.

One month later, after climbing a passageway with a slope of 32° they were able to enter into a rectangular room. The place had a ceiling in the shape of a two-sloped trestle, quite similar to those used to bury women's corpses (men's corpses were buried in a chamber with a horizontal roof). They thus named it the 'Chamber of the Queen'.

There they found an empty niche, which Al-Mamun believed to be the entrance to a gallery. He ordered the stonemasons to drill a hole in it, and a few hours later he was informed that it was useless to continue in that endeavour. They had managed to dig more than a metre (3 feet), but they only came upon stone that was even harder than the previous stone.

'The Chamber of the King'

When they left that place, two Arabs discovered a great cavity above their heads beyond the ascending passageway. They ran to tell the young caliph, who regained hope of finding a treasure. He thus ordered that this new path be explored.

However, this would not be an easy undertaking. The Arabs had to go up by standing on each others' shoulders, in a kind of human ladder, all of them carrying lit torches. After a few hours of strenuous efforts, they found a helping hand from scaffolding that allowed them to continue their climb. This is how they reached a gallery, 29 feet long, at the end of which they found another hollow in the ceiling.

Fortunately, this new one was not as complicated as the previous one, since it had notches in its walls where they could place their feet, although using great care, since the stone was quite slippery. Once they overcame this obstacle, they faced many others, some in the form of such low passageways that they had to crawl lying down. Finally, they saw a large room.

By torchlight they saw that the walls were made of reddish granite, well carved and polished. When Al-Mamun entered, he was told that the space measured 34.4 feet long, 17.3 feet wide and 19 feet high. They named it 'The Chamber of the King'.

A display of generosity

The entire large space was examined without leaving a single corner untouched in the hopes of finding some type of treasure. But there was only an enormous 'sarcophagus' without a lid, empty, exquisitely polished and carved in a chocolate-coloured granite. It was the only thing of value they found.

Well, Arab legends tell that Al-Mamun extracted the stone statue of a man from the coffin, which was the wrapping of a corpse covered with objects of immense value: a golden breastplate embedded with precious stones, a sword of incalculable value, and a ruby carbuncle the size of a hen's egg and as bright as the midday sun. It is also said that they found mysterious inscriptions in the coffin that no one could decipher.

The truth of the matter, according to historians, is different. At first, Al-Mamun believed that the Great Pyramid had been built to house an empty tomb; however, in the end he became convinced that someone had arrived before him to plunder the treasures. That is why he gave the order to abandon the work.

The Arab artisans were so enraged that they spent several hours banging their hammers on the beautiful granite walls in the 'Chamber of the King'. Nevertheless, as they left they found a chest full of ancient gold coins, which they brought to Al-Mamun, convinced that they were part of the treasures pillaged from the Great Pyramid. The young caliph authorised them to distribute the coins according to the professional standing of those who had taken part in the exploration.

Another legend says that this chest of ancient gold coins belonged to Al-Mamun himself, who showed such generosity in order to ease the feeling of failure that had spread among his people.

The great barbaric act

What happened in the following centuries gives us an idea that the Arabs considered this chest of ancient gold coins to be little reward compared to the colossal size of the Pyramid of Cheops. This is proven by the great barbaric act involved in tearing off the 22 acres of marble covering that was 8.2 feet thick. A large part of this material was used in the buildings of El Kaherah ('The Victorious One'), the new capital of the Arab kingdom. A mosque in Cairo was also built using this marble.

Likewise, major earthquakes covered the secret entrance discovered by Al-Mamun's men as well as the 98 feet gallery carved out by them. The sand blown by the wind also acted to gradually bury the sphinxes and the pyramids, and what remained visible of all of them were 'unusable' ruins which for many years were used, as we have already mentioned, by the Mameluks and other Arab tribes as targets for firearms.

The enigmatic Caviglia

The presence of Napoleon's armies in Egypt, which he had conquered, led to the pyramids' gaining the worldwide importance that they still have today. This was even truer when Champollion managed to decipher the Rosetta Stone, thus opening the door to knowledge about one of the most powerful, magical and mysterious civilisations the world has ever known.

Nevertheless, with the defeat of the 'Great Corsican' in Waterloo, one could say that Egypt lost part of the spotlight. Perhaps for this reason an enigmatic personage from Genoa named Caviglia was able to act as he pleased. One of his contemporaries described him in this way:

He was so passionate about what he called "the temple of ancient science and magic" that he did not mind sacrificing his country, his house, his family, his friends and his fortune. All to satisfy his refined taste, which I consider eccentric, for exploring the mysteries that must be hidden in the pyramids and tombs of Egypt.

Caviglia stayed near the Great Pyramid, just as one who wanted to convert the place into his own home would. He hired a good team of skilled workers and began to clear the entrances to the monument, since the secret discovered by Al-Mamun had been revealed by other researchers before him. He then devoted himself to exploring as a fanatic would, although without failing to adhere to a meticulous order.

Nor did he ever forget to say his prayers, eat at the set time and keep himself clean. Since he believed in human beings' magical powers, hypnotism and animal magnetism preached by Mesmer, he was convinced that the colossal monument would provide him with great discoveries.

He attempted to discover them using the paths opened by other French and English researchers, until he became convinced that he would not achieve any positive results. This led him to go down a well almost 131 feet deep in the hope

102

that this would help him find a new route, an undertaking that became very complicated and dangerous since the air became unbreathable at the bottom, the torches could barely remain lit from the lack of oxygen and the bottom appeared to be a dead end.

Nevertheless, Caviglia doubled his Arab workers' pay so that they would continue to work. From the well, they extracted hundreds of baskets of earth until hard rock was struck. Since breathing continued to be impossible at the bottom, perhaps due to the enormous amount of bat excrement more than the lack of air, the enigmatic Genovese man had to give up, although he did not give up the exploration altogether, since he had yet another possibility: clearing a descending passageway that must have connected with the bottom of the well.

This work took more than one week. Finally, Caviglia himself entered a very narrow passageway, crawling forward approximately 147 feet. The air was rarefied and there was so much dust that at times he even spat out blood, although this did not stop him. Such effort was rewarded by finding a very promising narrow opening.

When the Arabs penetrated it, they could all smell sulphur. This told them that they were near the well. And when they continued to dig, a current of clean, fresh air reached them. They had just found one of the ventilation systems built by the ancient Egyptians. Nevertheless, they were not able to continue carving at the bottom of the well due to the hardness of the rock.

Dynamite to open the way

Around the same time Richard Howard-Vyse arrived in the area. He was an officer of the British guard, son of General Richard Vyse and grandson of the Count of Stafford. Since he was a very rich man, he hired more workers than anybody else and made Caviglia head of the large group.

As the enigmatic Genovese had fascinated him with his stories, he let him continue his explorations while he "went around the Nile to take a look at the other Pyramids". The truth is that this Englishman loved fun, so much so that his wealthy family had sent him to Egypt with plenty of pounds sterling in order to "get rid of him".

From this moment on, the military man devoted himself to exploring the inside of the Great Pyramid with such enthusiasm that he was willing to use gunpowder when faced with a large obstacle. This decision made him the worst of the plunderers. He had hired an Arab specialist for this mission, named Daueh, who was said to sustain himself exclusively on hashish and wine.

But he cannot have been too drunk when he introduced the cartridges into a crack, lit the fuse and waited for the explosion. Despite the fact that the stone splinters shot out like battering rams capable of taking off the heads, legs or arms of whomever they struck, there was not a single tragedy, except for the damage caused to the Great Pyramid. Moreover, they had access to a new chamber, which Howard-Vyse named 'Wellington' in honour of the English general that had defeated Napoleon.

Its floor was made up of eight granite ashlars, each weighing more than fifty tonnes. What is most interesting is the fact that the intruders were greeted by a rain of black dust, which left them looking like coal miners, because although the bats had not been able to enter there in order to fill it with their excrement, thousands of insects had, and their skeletons and shells had turned into dust after having passed through a stage of petrifaction. Not a single insect was found alive.

As the months went by, Howard-Vyse would find four more chambers which he named after different English famous people. The most important thing is that in one of them inscriptions were found from the time of Khufu, the second pharaoh in the fourth dynasty, whom the Greeks named Cheops or Keops.

Two great discoveries

Howard-Vyse noted the existence of two holes in the ceiling of the Chamber of the King which had already drawn the attention of other researchers. But on this occasion Mr Hill was there, one of the Colonel's helpers after having been the manager of a hotel in Cairo. As a very determined individual, he climbed one of the walls of the Great Pyramid until finding the two entryways. He soon opened them, and during the following days, cleared more then 229 feet of ventilation ducts.

Once this was done, it could be seen that the temperature in the Chamber of the King, which had been asphyxiating, went down to 20° and did not change all day. With time it was seen that it did not change with the different seasons either, nor with wind storms. This proved some researchers' theories that this site had been used by the ancient Egyptians as an archive for weights and measures, which need to have stable temperatures and barometric pressure.

Another great discovery by this colonel, who used gunpowder cartridges again on other occasions, were the two polished marble panels he found on the north façade of the Great Pyramid, precisely at one of its bases. The fact that he had ordered the pyramid to be cleared away allowed him to demonstrate that all the stories told about the beautiful covering on the Pyramid were true.

The panels measured 4.9 feet high, 12 feet long and 8 feet wide. They were sloped at 51° 51', had been cut on an exact angle and were as highly polished as an optical instrument. Since this was a true archaeological treasure, Howard-Vyse ordered them to be covered until they could be transported to England.

However, a few days later a group of Arabs broke the panels, *because the Christians will never take out of Egypt what belongs to Muslims*, yet another barbarous act that the English colonel greatly regretted. But he had enough information, as well as numerous drawings of his findings. With all this, he was able to publish two books which his family financed, with the titles *Operations Carried on at the Pyramids of Gizeh in 1837*. One of his helpers, John Perring, also wrote the book called *The Pyramids of Gizeh from Actual Survey and Measurement on the 1839-1842 Spot*.

Another of the misfortunes accompanying Howard-Vyse's work was the loss of Menkaure's sarcophagus, which had been extracted from the third pyramid he explored. The boat transporting it sank along the Spanish coast in a storm. Far from being branded a plunderer, the work by Colonel Howard-Vyse, along with the work written by his helper, generated great excitement, so much so that a new discipline, called 'Pyramidology', was created.

Chapter IX

THE SCIENTIFIC THEORIES

A unique researcher

Twentieth-century westerners were quite enamoured with ancient Egypt; thus, their museums, their nobility and their most important cities wished to have some important testimony of such an exotic civilisation. Everyone wanted to have his own mummy; obelisks were installed in the most unlikely places; decorators filled walls and furniture with sphinxes and crocodiles; and works on the subject proliferated.

This passion reached such a pitch that the Scottish peer Alexander, tenth Duke of Hamilton, ordered his corpse to be mummified. In the United States, a city in Tennessee was named Memphis in memory of an ancient coastal Egyptian town. And in 1880, an obelisk called 'Cleopatra's Needle' was erected in New York's Central Park.

Perhaps England was the country that brought a more practical sense to all this admiration, since they were questioning many things, especially in the religious context. Thus they attempted to see in the pyramids the best evidence for the existence of God.

One of the best examples of this idea can be found in the unique researcher, John Taylor, who was a learned man in holy writings, director of the "London Magazine", mathematician, astrologer and man of letters. Despite the fact that he had a wide circle of friends, almost all of them very important, he asked none of them for advice when taking a vital decision to research the Great Pyramid.

But he did not travel to Egypt, which would have been the most logical, rather he immersed himself in an enormous study. Right there he built a scaled replica of the Pyramid of Cheops, brought together the greatest amount of information possible, and began his studies. Previously he had made sure to have all the documentation possible, much of which was sent from Egypt itself.

Some interesting surprises

Months later, he began to make some verifications that caused great surprise: each time he multiplied the perimeter of the Pyramid by two times its height, the result was almost the absolute value of *pi*: 3.14159+. We all know that this is the value that must be multiplied by the diameter of a circle in order to calculate its circumference.

To say that Taylor trembled when he finished making these verifications would be to understate his mood, because he had just discovered that the ancient Egyptians knew the value of *pi*, while until then it had been believed that it was a discovery dating from the sixth century AD. This led him to sense that he was entering a disturbing world, because he had just seen the first sign of the science of the builders of the pyramids. But what else could he find out?

Taylor did not doubt that the ancient Egyptians had at least managed to measure the circumference of the Earth and the distance between the centre of the Earth and the poles. Later he would come upon other very interesting surprises: the relationship between the height of the pyramid and its perimeter was identical to the polar radius of the Earth with its circumference: 2 *pi*: This geometric knowledge seemed to the erudite Englishman so wonderful that he refused to attribute it to wise men from antiquity. Thus he wrote:

We have to assume that in the early ages of history, the Creator allowed a group of human beings to possess such an intellectual capacity that it would lead them to carry out works that would be far beyond those achieved by future inhabitants of our planet. Thus they knew how to build the pyramids, just as earlier Noah had been able to construct the Arc following God's advice...

Taylor dared to propose the hypothesis that the architects of the pyramids belonged to a 'chosen' race from the line of Abraham, albeit before him. He put them closer to Noah. Likewise, since their geometrical calculations had allowed him to check that the 'pyramidal inch', as he called the measure used by the ancient Egyptians, was so similar to the English inch, he dared to venture the idea that his compatriots, that is, people born in England, were related to some of the lost tribes of Israel, *who conserved the wisdom of the Egyptians.*

But this scientist was already more than sixty years old, which meant that the Royal Society, before which he presented his studies, considered them more fitting for the Society of Antiquaries. We should bear in mind that the English nation had already been shaken by the scandal of Darwin's theories on the origin of the species. Surely nobody wanted to provoke another cultural conflict. But Taylor was not discouraged, so in 1859 he decided to publish his book, *The Great Pyramid: Why was it Built and Who Built it?*

The most passionate follower

John Taylor received a very comforting visit just when he believed that nobody supported his ideas: Professor Charles Piazzi Smyth, a royal astronomer from Scotland. Just on exchanging their first words, the elder gentleman realized that he had before him a passionate follower, an admirer who asked the most penetrating questions and to whom it was worth providing more information than that contained in his book.

Smyth was the son of an admiral and godson of one of the most famous astronomers of the time: the Italian, Giuseppe Piazzi, who had discovered the first asteroid. But the academic and professional merits of Taylor's admirer were not only in his family, since he himself had achieved the position of royal astronomer when he was only twenty-six years old. In addition, he was a member of the 'Royal Society of Edinburgh', one of the most prestigious institutions in the country, as a result of his studies on optics. Nevertheless, when they heard that he wished to travel to Egypt to verify Taylor's theories *in situ*, many people tried to discourage him since they viewed this research as inappropriate for a scientist of his calibre.

But no one managed to get the forty-five-year-old astronomer to reconsider. Thus he left England at the end of 1864 with his wife. The equipment he took consisted of the best measuring devices, cameras, and a complete set of astronomic instruments. Nor did he forget certain amenities, such as hammocks, chairs and large tents.

Upon his first observations, Smyth could see that the Great Pyramid was a few minutes off latitude thirty degrees north. He also discovered that the shadow of this monument totally disappeared during the spring equinox, which led him to the idea that the Egyptian architects possessed great knowledge of astronomy. As he expected, he also verified that Taylor's measurements were almost exact, so he took pains to improve on them.

Another matter on which he agreed with his admired master was the religious aspect, despite the fact that he accepted the idea that he was before *the most extraordinary work that human beings could have made throughout history*. What he had before him was a work of God, which is why its measurements were so astonishing: the perimeter of the monument's structure in pyramidal inches was similar to 1,000 times 365.2, the number of days in the solar year, meaning that the ancient Egyptians had anticipated the Greeks, to whom this calculation had been attributed, by fifteen centuries.

After many months of research, Smyth reached the conclusion that *the Bible tells us that in previous ages God gave wisdom and metric instructions to a few human beings in order for them to build buildings, always through some kind of special, mysterious intervention*. He also claimed that the pyramid revealed the distance between the Earth and the Sun, just as it predicted the date of Jesus Christ's second coming.

These ideas created a large number of enemies for the astronomer, some of whom even ridiculed him. However, just as happened earlier to John Taylor, they also served to gain him some admirers in different parts of the world, as he could see when he started to receive letters encouraging him to continue his research and requesting additional information and advice.

The embryo of great theories

It could be said that Taylor's and Smyth's writing started the race for the broadest type of research. As the Great Pyramid was being studied, the spiritual messages enclosed within it were discovered, as were those relating to history. In 1877, the American priest, Joseph Seiss, wrote:

The stones of the pyramids offer an immense system of inter-related numbers, measurements, weights, angles, temperatures, degrees, geometric problems and cosmic references.

Seiss was also impressed by the fact that the number five was so frequently repeated in the pyramid: five corners, five sides (including the base), and the pyramidal inch consisted of one-fifth of the fifth of a cube. Thus he wondered: *Is this a simple coincidence, if we bear in mind that we have five senses, five fingers on each limb and five of Moses' books were found?*

He then saw that the longitude and latitude coordinates (thirty-one degrees east and thirty degrees north), which crossed on the land occupied by the Great Pyramid covered a greater area of land than any other conjunction of similar lines. He thus had to ask the question: *Did the ancient Egyptians know that they were building in the exact centre of the world populated at that time?*

Also, if a straight-lined quadrant was drawn from the Pyramid toward the northeast and northwest, the entire Nile Valley could be covered, a measurement that must have been quite useful to Egyptian architects, especially when the river that gave them life was in flood, which made calculations impossible.

Nevertheless, once again the pressure groups most attacked the established religious doctrines: the evolutionists to support their ideas, since if one accepted Darwin's theories on the origins of man coming from 'a simian with the ability to perfect itself', they were willing to back the most avant-garde ideas; meanwhile, the Catholic fundamentalists refused to tolerate someone attempting to change the Bible's message and that of the other holy texts.

Since the established idea on the beginning of the world was the year 4004 BC, (calculated by the Irish religious man James Usher in the eighteenth century), the fact that the pyramids were this old forced people to accept the theory that the Egyptian architects were the first inhabitants, and not primitive hunters with no further knowledge than how to survive using the most elementary means, since they did not know how to use fire.

If the architects who built the pyramids were the first inhabitants of the Earth, there was no doubt that God had created them in his image and likeness: privileged bodies and minds, ready to build and produce inconceivable wonders, a minimal part of which were coming to light at that time. Since this theory did not seem so extreme, at least for some members of western society, in the United States an organisation whose main mission was to defend a system of measurement based on the holy cubits of the pyramid was created, rejecting the metric system because they considered it atheist. President James Gardfield was a member of this organisation.

The scientists who questioned some 'truths'

Some people might have supported the idea that the research on the pyramids should be done by someone who did not belong to one of the most well-known religions, or at least who was least affected by them. The fact is, in 1880, the Englishman, William Matthew Flinders Petrie, went to Egypt aiming to make the most exact measurements.

Flinders Petrie was not an unknown. His grandfather had organised major expeditions in Australia, while his father was interested in continuing Taylor's and Smyth's investigations.

112

Since his father was an engineer with a solid reputation, before embarking on an endeavour that he considered so important he commissioned special measuring instruments to be made. But he had been involved in this matter for more than twenty years.

Meanwhile his son, Flinders Petrie, had completed the trade of topographer, whose knowledge he broadened by setting out to measure a large number of religious buildings in England and Scotland. He also went to some megalithic sites, like the enormous stone circles at Stonehenge. And when he felt prepared, he decided to travel to the pyramids of Egypt before his father.

Once he was on the Giza plateau, he realized that tourists were going to make his research difficult. In order to shock them, he went around half-naked, horrifying the Victorian women who ran away as soon as they saw him. Nevertheless, since this was not very successful, he had to get used to working at night despite the fact that he ran great risks, such as happened to his friend, Doctor Grant, who fell into a well more than 2.5 feet deep with no wall supports. He thus had to get him out by lifting him onto his back and attempting to jump to grab onto something outside the well, which allowed him to pull himself up.

Beyond these difficulties, Flinders Petrie confirmed the precision of the work done, especially in the realm of the stones' fit. It seemed to him to be *the work of a divine optician, whom not even a thousandth of an inch of error had escaped*. In addition, he saw that the walls of the passageway through which he descended to the pharaoh's sarcophagus only had one-fourth of an inch of unevenness in its 347 feet of length.

Petrie published the results of his research in the book *The Pyramids and Temples of Gizeh*. He had discovered that there was a relationship of *pi* in the length and periphery in the Chamber of the King. However, the calculations he made on the base of the pyramid were smaller than those given by Smyth, thus discarding the idea that this measurement represented the number of days in the solar year.

Since Petrie's studies were taken more seriously, due to English society's assimilation of the old cultural scandals, the queen granted him the title of Sir. With this, 'Egyptology' or 'Pyramidology' became accepted sciences, so much so that magazines devoted solely to this topic started to be published.

The engineer who set out to destroy the fantasies

The engineer, Donald Davidson, born in the English town of Leeds, an agnostic and an important builder, wished to destroy all the fantasies about Egypt, especially Robert Menzies' idea that the pyramids' passageways revealed prophecies about the most important events in universal history.

Two weeks after beginning his studies in the Great Pyramid, he had to admit that the calculations, declarations and theories were based on evidence that could not be argued. Their interpretation was different; but, all the geometric and mathematical data coincided with his.

A few months in Egypt convinced Davidson that he had to accept this principle: *the Pyramid is an expression of God's Truth in structural form, which confirms the fact that the Bible is a book inspired by divine will*, something that coming from an agnostic must have been quite shocking at that time.

Since this engineer was not someone who would settle for one or two pieces of proof, he repeated all his calculations and measurements. The results obtained led him to confirm the data provided by John Taylor, while it also supported his theories: *the ancient Egyptians' science and system of weights and measures was based on two functions of the Earth and its orbit: the basic unit of time was the solar year, while the linear must be viewed as a decimal fraction of the polar axis on which our planet rotates.*

Davidson did more than this, since he found the way to bring Smyth's and Petrie's theories in line with each other. Having discovered that the internal mass of the ashlars on each side of the pyramid was concave, which could not be seen by the naked eye, he made a different calculation of the pyramid's base, based on a deformation produced by the passage of time. Thus the measurement of the base did in fact correspond with the solar year. He explained it in this way:

Due to this minor omission, some scientists had assumed

114

that the theory of the deceased Royal Astronomer of Scotland, the great Professor Piazzi Smyth, who gave the base of the Great Pyramid the measurement of 36,524 inches, could only be considered fantasy. Yet it was not, since he told us that each side of the base measured 9,131.5 pyramidal inches or 9,131.1 English inches, which in reality is 9,141.4, which means a slight error by a third of an inch, something that contradicts neither his calculations nor his ideas.

Davidson's own theories

Donald Davidson's own theories on all these matters must be seen: the fact that the pyramid's sides were concave provided three main lengths in the year, which could be seen in its base: a smaller exterior, measured from one side to the other without considering the concavity; another, a little longer, to which we add a part of the depression that the four sides produced over the base; and a third one, which corresponds to the entirety of the angles within the face. The three measurements made by the ancient Egyptians would have produced the three lengths in the year that have been calculated by modern-day science: the solar year, the astral year, and anomalous years, each one depending on the system used to make the observation.

Based on these theories, pyramidologists from all over the world had to modify their concepts. They also organised new schools, some of which operated on into the twentieth century.

A highly original theory

In 1919, D. Neroman, President of the French College of Astrologers, a mine engineer by profession, published his book *La Clè Secrète de la Pyramide* (*The Secret Key of the Pyramid*). In the book, he tried to demonstrate that the holy cubit used by Smyth and the royal cubit used by Petrie were linked by a mathematical relationship. He also proved that the pyramid had the height and thickness needed for the calculations to provide an exact number of each unit. Given that thirty-three holy cubits equalled forty royal or common cubits, the base provided a measurement of four hundred and forty royal cubits or three hundred and sixty-three holy cubits; and the height, two hundred and eighty or two hundred and twenty-one, a set of data that rather than being contradictory is complementary.

Some of the readers of this work proposed the idea that the Egyptian architects, or the initiates, measured the length of the solar year using a holy cubit, since only they were able to use the secret science of the pyramid.

Another highly original theory was set forth by John B. Schmaltz in his work *Nuggets from King Solomon's Mines*. In his opinion, the modern deck of cards might have been created using the Egyptian solar year as a reference, calculated by measuring the Great Pyramid. Thus he claimed the following:

The fifty-two cards must represent the weeks: the twelve figures, the months; the thirteen cards in each suit, the lunar cycles; and the four suits, the seasons. In addition, the total sum of the cards (assigning the jack number eleven; the queen number twelve and the king number thirteen) would produce the three hundred sixty-four days, to which we must add the joker as the magical figure of 1.2334, thus reaching a total of 365.234 days per year.

Davidson defends his theories

Since Donald Davidson's theories were continuously questioned by important men of science, Morton Edgar travelled to Egypt, in 1912, with the sole purpose of defending the much-admired engineer. Among the calculations he made on the Great Pyramid, we must emphasize those relating to the twenty-fifth row. He confirmed that it was a little thicker than the others, which must be understood as the datum that provided the measurement of the equinoxes.

But this did not serve to eliminate the controversies, since it was said that if the value of *pi* had been applied to the pyramid, while its base had been calculated to reach

365.2322 cubits long, it would have been impossible for its diagonals to indicate the length with such precision as claimed by the Egyptologists.

To this Donald Davidson replied, always in defence of his theory, that the architects of the pyramids knew all the derivations of the natural laws; nevertheless, to understand their designs and calculations one had to reduce the astronomical properties of the solar year to a simple pyramidal expression. Because it was quite clear that when calculating the distance of the Earth to the Sun, as well as the length of the astral year in seconds, it was easy to calculate the speed of the Earth's rotation around the sun, as well as finding out the specific gravity of our planet, the Sun, the Moon and the speed of light. And he concluded using these words:

To me it has become very clear that Egyptian civilisation was much more knowledgeable and well-documented than ours in the science of gravitational astronomy and thus in the mathematical foundations of the mechanical arts and sciences, because human beings have taken thousands of years to discover through experiments what was already known through a more reliable, safe and simple system. This means that all of modern civilisation's empirical knowledge is a provisional collection of hypotheses compared to the foundations of the natural law of Egyptian civilisation.

When Davidson was asked how the Egyptian architects had delineated all the galleries and passageways inside the Great Pyramid with such precision, his response was this blunt:

The ancient wise men wanted to provide a monument to the science of their time, in order for it to be discovered by a faraway civilisation. Since they were convinced that their knowledge might disappear, due to their own extinction before the common beings would learn it, they created this gigantic secret library. Another of their goals was to pique the interest of future civilisations, which is what is taking place now, as they discover the great wisdom enclosed in the stone.

Nevertheless, just as had happened earlier to Menzies and Smyth, the only thing Davidson managed to do was enrage the more traditional scientific world. He also displeased those

117

who awaited confirmation of the magic and religiosity of ancient Egypt, because his claim that the pyramids were nothing more than a means of passing on data, just like a monumental library, did not satisfy many people. In reality, the works of this researcher provided a large amount of data that nobody was capable of refuting. It is true that they served to encourage many other scientists, especially those who were sure that the history of the world, from its origins to its end, could be found hidden in the pyramids' underground galleries.

But this is a matter that deserves a chapter of its own.

Chapter X

THE PROPHECIES OF THE PYRAMIDS

The first supporters of the Prophecies

At the beginning of the twentieth century, different pyramidologists attempted to prove that the Great Pyramid of Cheops held the prophetic history of the world throughout six thousand years; thus it began in 4000 BC and ended in 2045 AD, coinciding with the prophecies in the Bible.

For all these people, the pyramid was a stone allegory, since its descending galleries represented human beings in their declining road toward ignorance and perdition. At the convergence of the ascending passageways, the malign spirits would continue to the well, while the rest of humanity, protected by Christianity, kept climbing this passageway in search of the light in the Great Gallery. After overcoming the enormous step, all human beings would continue, prostrate and without will, until they arrived at the antechamber of confusion (representation of the modern age), in order to reach the Chamber of the King, where they would arrive once they felt free, because they would have entered the paradise of the second coming.

It was said that all the prophetic chronologies were indicated in the underground passageways and the inside chambers, with each year corresponding to a pyramidal inch. It began with the presence of Adam and Eve in Paradise, that is, the first human beings created, and ended on the Final Judgement Day.

Following what was written by Morton Edgar, the admirer of Donald Davidson's theories, *Judgement Day will arrive toward the year 2914, so that all human beings shall benefit from Jesus Christ's sacrifice. From then on the purity of human nature which our first father Adam lost 7,040 years before when he disobeyed the Lord's commandments shall be recovered.*

All the supporters of the prophecies agreed that the lower passageway, the one that led to the antechamber, marked the beginning of the First World War in 1914. They also believed that the end of the Chamber of the King referred to certain events that would occur in 1953.

Certain clarifications are needed

Many Egyptologists support the idea that thousands of prophecies are contained in the Great Pyramid; nevertheless, they are well aware that the passage of time has worn down the stone, moved some of the blocks and altered almost all the references. This means that we must bear these modifications in mind when interpreting the signals left by the initiates.

Another clarification that should be made is that we are not talking about prophecies like those of Nostradamus or other wise men, but a type of announcement of inevitable events, such as great cataclysms or cosmic movements whose consequences for humanity are very far from being anticipated by current science. They also refer to the prophecies of superior events.

Robert Menzies is one of the pyramidologists that has discussed the matter of the Great Pyramid's prophecies; however, his viewpoint is affected by his Christian education, which leads him to relate the dimensions of the great gallery, always measured in holy inches, with the western chronology, taking Jesus Christ's birth as a reference. Thus, he located the beginning of the two world wars in the twentieth century, which had been mentioned in the Bible, in the Lower Passageway of the antechamber.

The initiate Georges Barbarin

Georges Barbarin is one of the scholars that has most prolifically written on the prophecies of the Pyramid of Cheops. Perhaps he is also one of the most daring, one who does not mind 'playing with fire' because he is convinced that he is handling truth. Let us examine some of his references:

The date of the Nativity is given by the location of the floor of the Chamber of the Queen, which the ancient ones called the 'the Chamber of the Second and New Birth'.

Jesus came into the world in the year 4 AD (which would be year 3996 in terms of the Pyramid), which was the Festival of the Tabernacles, corresponding to the 15th of the month of Tisri, which was related with Saturday the 4th in the Gregorian calendar.

For those who are astonished that this day does not coincide with the Nativity, it is necessary to clarify the fact that 25th December has been, since ancient times, a festival of pagan origin celebrating the birth of the invisible sun, which, until the third century AD was known by the name 'Natalis solis invicti.' On this day homage was paid to the winter solstice...

...The date of the crucifixion can be located at the threshold of the Great Gallery. This date is highly important if we bear in mind that the Egyptian sacred texts identified this place with the 'age of the Saviour of Humankind'. At the same time, the Great Gallery became the symbol of the Christian era, which began with Jesus Christ's death and resurrection.

It is worth emphasizing the fact that all the symbolism existing in the life of Jesus Christ is constantly confused with the symbolism of the Great Pyramid itself... Thus at the threshold of the Great Gallery we can read that the date of the Crucifixion was precisely Friday, the 7th April in the year 340, in accordance with the Julian calendar (the 15th of the Hebrew month of Nisan).

...In accordance with the references given to us by the pyramid, which are backed by the "Book of the Dead", the years of Chaos cover from the entrance to the First Lower Passageway to the doorway of the Chamber of the King. This

corresponds to the 4th-5th August, 1914 until the 15th-16th September, 1936.

This time of desolation for humanity (which resembles Jacob's Trouble from the Bible) is obvious from the fact that it is virtually impossible to walk upright in the lower passageways since they are no higher than a metre unless one bends down or crawls, if very tall.

We are referring to a period in which it was quite difficult to make progress. The obstacles are found in the Lower Passageways, near the Antechamber. From there on one can stand up again, meaning, according to the interpretations from the "Book of the Dead", that the Truce of Chaos has been reached. But it will be necessary to bend down once again to pass below the granite panel.

This period of chaos has three different parts:

1. From the threshold of the First Lower Passageway until reaching its end (pyramidal dates: the 4th-5th August, 1914 to the 10th-11th November, 1918).

2. The length of the Antechamber until reaching the entrance to the Second Lower Passageway (pyramidal dates: the 10th November, 1918 until the 28th-29th May, 1928).

3. From the entrance to the Second Lower Passageway to the end of it, which is also the entrance to the Chamber of the King (pyramidal dates: the 29th May, 1928 to the 15th-16th September, 1936).

We shall see how the chaotic periods also happen in this way:

a) From the beginning of World War I until the signing of the armistice.

b) From the armistice until the world economic crisis.

c) From the world crisis until the theocratic age or spiritual reappearance, which is framed in the entrance to the Chamber of the King itself...

As can be seen, the interpretation of the signs, configurations and sizes of the underground passageways, entrances and rooms are within the reach of highly learned people. We must consider Georges Barbarin, as well as the other pyramidologists who have been capable of reading the prophecies, as initiates.

The future Prophecies

A few years ago, Peter Lemesurier, published the book *The Great Pyramid Decoded,* in the pages of which he dared to condense the majority of the prophecies found in this gigantic stone library. Nevertheless, he provided a highly original piece of information when he presented the figure of the 'Great Initiate', who would be in charge of leading the human beings, or 'lesser initiates', through extensive spiritual paths throughout many ages.

Since what interests us in this book are the prophecies relating to our future, let us summarise some of them:

2034: the 'precursor' to the Messiah shall emerge.

2039: the beginning of the second appearance of the Messiah on earth.

2076: beginning of the age of superior consciousness, which as it expands will allow all of humanity to elevate itself to levels of great experience.

2116: the Messiah shall leave this plane of existence.

2132-2133: the possibility of spiritual escape for those human beings who have not been able to reach the required degree of enlightenment shall be exhausted.

2134: the third coming of the Messiah on earth. The enlightened ones shall no longer succumb to falling into a phase of spiritual darkness because of error or failure.

2138: the Messiah shall abandon the earthly plane. The bases of human existence shall be reaffirmed.

2264: fourth coming of the Messiah to earth.

2279: those who are partially enlightened shall begin to be initiated into superior learning.

2368: the Messiah shall leave this plane of existence.

2394: fifth and last coming of the Messiah to earth.

2422 to 2477: last efforts to attempt reform those who lack complete enlightenment...

6225: those who have just been enlightened shall leave the material plane and enter into a period of reward, which they shall find on the spiritual plane. But they shall continue to maintain certain ties to the earth.

7267: beginning of the Second High Millennium. Those who have been recently enlightened return to the physical world for the last time in order to prepare for their permanent departure from the earthly plane.

8276: end of the Second High Millennium. Those who have just been enlightened shall leave the earth forever in order to join the enlightened souls who have already reached the first of the purely spiritual planes...

According to the prophecies as interpreted by Lemesurier, always taking the Great Pyramid as a reference point, in the year 8400, the Earth shall be empty; its cycle of existence will have ended. Meanwhile, the souls of all of humanity shall not stop progressing in other dimensions, where nothing can be measured by the parameters of time and space, in a zone where there are five levels of spiritual experience, all of which lead to the great final step.

At this time the Messiah's plans with regard to the evolution of the human race shall have been fulfilled, as can be seen by the fact that the souls shall go from a finite plane to an infinite one. The moment will have come when they return to the place they came from: God's own mind.

Chapter XI

THE ALBUM OF THE AGES

An immense sundial

One of the verifications that Smyth made when studying the Great Pyramid was that, with the arrival of spring, at the moment when the Sun was very high in the sky, the entire north zone of the monument was illuminated. Since at mid-day shadows are foreshortened, this led him to assume that the Egyptian architects wished also for the Pyramid to fulfil the functions of a gigantic sundial, one so complete that it could give information on the seasons and the length of the year.

The Pyramid was intentionally built in this place – wrote Smyth – *where it had a slope and an orientation so that this phenomenon would take place on the spring equinox, precisely at the moment when the midday Sun was directly over the equator, despite the fact that for some reason that I do not know this phenomenon could not be seen with such precision at that time...*

Uniquely, the French astronomer Jean-Baptiste Biot, who had visited Egypt, in 1853, had made very similar verifications years earlier, something that Smyth was not aware of. Let us see what the French astronomer believed:

I do not know if this was the Egyptian architects' intention, but since it was finished the Great Pyramid has always acted

125

as a fabulous solar quadrant through which one can deter-
mine the phases of length of the equinoxes with an error of
less than a day, as well as those of the solstices, but these with
a margin of error of one and three-quarter days...

The desire to change the current calendar

The previous studies attracted the interest of Moses B. Cotsworth, an unknown lawyer in the English county of Yorkshire. One of his dreams was to reform the current calendar, since it seemed absurd to him to maintain it when its origin was Roman and it had led to so many errors throughout time.

Cotsworth had felt so fascinated by the fact that the Great Pyramid might be an album or almanac of the ages in which the years were recorded, that he completely devoted himself to confirming this.

He soon realized that any obelisk located at the same latitude as the Pyramid could also show the time of day or the passage of the seasons with great exactness; nonetheless, they could never be tall enough to provide the length of the entire year consisting of three hundred and sixty-five days, nor to add another one-fourth of a day until reaching ten-thousandths.

The Great Pyramid could do this. Thus, Cotsworth believed that this monument could help him measure the six winter months, when its northern face remained totally in the shade, leading to its midday projection over the northern ground to be prolonged much more in the southern direction. It would do this until reaching its greatest size in the winter solstice, and would gradually wane until it disappeared completely midday on some date in March.

In defence of the astronomical theories

Cotsworth was demonstrating great tenacity, and he decided to meet with Piazzi Smyth in 1900. But he found him on his deathbed, although that did not prevent them from having some very interesting conversations. This led to the lawyer to buy all the books and papers of the much-admired researcher once they were auctioned off after his death. He had waited for more than a year, since he had good informants, and the most opportune moment arrived.

He studied all this material for several months. In the end he did not agree with some of Smyth's theories, but he did with all his astronomical references. He thus devoted himself to reconstructing the sundial in accordance with the calculations, dimensions and orientation of the Great Pyramid.

In his studio, he built various pyramids and cones which he placed on meticulously diagrammed papers. These enabled him to measure the shadows every half-hour over several months in order to reach the conclusion that he was on the right track. The pyramid was a perfect form, better than the cone since it could be oriented toward the north, it provided better-defined shadows and its height was precise. He captured this idea using these words:

The ancient Egyptian architects raised the Great Pyramid on an ideal surface, in which the shadows were projected over a meridian line oriented toward the north. They also made sure that it had geometrical proportions, which aided them in measuring the shadows more accurately.

For a structure 448 feet high, such as Pyramid of Cheops, they had to prepare a projection surface that would extend about 268 feet toward the north of the base, in order for the entire shadow to fit, even at its longest, at the December solstice...

The best way of proving a theory

This volunteer researcher left for Port Said in November, 1900. He brought all the most modern instruments in order to make precise calculations. After a few days working on the Giza plateau, he congratulated himself for having found the Great Pyramid free of crags, just as the rocky surface appeared as smooth as he thought it needed to be. He had already located the 'projection surface' along the main platform which reached as far as the ruins of an old wall. He imagined that this wall surrounded the pyramid in ancient times.

What most reassured Cotsworth was discovering that the ground was divided into a type of half-squares, which provided him with twice as many points of union as he needed to measure the pyramid's shadow; an operation that he began to undertake along the south on the following mid-days, always taking care that the tourists did not bother him.

He also used a camera for assistance, which recorded the waning of the shadows in the direction of the spring equinox. Another happy moment arrived when he observed that the ashlars at the base had been cut to a thickness very close to the measure of 4.45 feet, which made the midday shadow continue the one from the day before approaching the moment of its disappearance in March.

More modern verifications

The confirmation that the Great Pyramid of Cheops had been built at a slight incline so that it could mark the moment of the equinox was verified, in 1934, by Andre Pochan. He managed to photograph the southern face of the monument using an infrared filter at 6 a.m. and 6 p.m. on the spring equinox.

That was how Pochan proved that, just as Petrie and Davidson had seen before, the northern and southern faces of the Great Pyramid could be used to indicate with the utmost accuracy the exact moment of the equinox. For this reason, on the morning of the equinox, when the sun's rays hit the southern face, the western half began to be illuminated. Later, as the sun set, the same phenomenon could be observed on the eastern half. In the period from the 21st March to the 21st June, this phenomenon could be seen for a short period of time, although only in mid-morning and long before sunset.

Certain modifications of the theory

But Cotsworth was not content to simply make observations on the Great Pyramid. Since he was in the place he loved, he decided to examine other pyramids, such as those of Saqqara, Maidum and Dashur. This led him to make certain modifications in his theories. For example, he started to believe that the Egyptian architects should not have oriented themselves using the equinox, when the Sun was in mid-path, but using the summer solstice, at the very moment when the Sun was at the highest point in the sky, that is, midday.

Since he also noticed different variations among the pyramids, he ended up offering the following hypothesis: *The ancient Egyptians were progressing northwards, until they reached the true pyramidal shape, that is, that provided by* pi, *in the thirteenth parallel, when the morning and afternoon shadows make completely straight lines.*

The pyramids were not the only almanacs of the ages

Cotsworth's idea was supported by renowned astronomers who had reached similar conclusions when observing other ancient monuments spread throughout Europe. The idea that these buildings were made to be albums or almanacs of time, days and years was clearly expressed by Peter Tompkins in his book "Secrets of the Great Pyramid":

Since we currently have all types of cheap clocks, television ads and calendars in the newspapers, we tend not to consider the value of having an exact means of measurement, a type of almanac of the ages which would indicate to them the day, the season and the year, for ancient civilisations. This is especially true for the Egyptians, all of whose agricultural work took place in accordance with the flooding of the Nile, which watered and fertilised the arable lands.

Every year, the Egyptian farmers would leave their villages, well protected in the mountains for three quarters of the year, in order to descend to the lowlands. They went with their families and livestock, and they also took the majority of their belongings. They worked the land, sowing and gathering crops. When the time came to return to the mountains with their families and goods, they had to know the exact date at least fifteen days in advance. Staying longer in the low-

lying area could mean their becoming isolated and thus per-
ishing in the annual floods from river waters. This had hap-
pened in ancient times, so they needed an accurate means of
avoiding it.

According to Cotsworth's calculation, all the efforts devoted
to learning the number of days in the year through the natural
signs of the seasons could only provide somewhat unreliable
results. In the earliest Egyptian dynasties, it was believed that
the flood of the Nile was announced by the annual heliacal
appearance of Sirius, which they called 'the dog star'.

Once a year, with the first blazes of dawn, this bright first-
magnitude star peeked out from the east, to dominate the
width of the sky until its brilliance was overcome by the ris-
ing sun. This amazing phenomenon was interpreted by the
ancient Egyptians as an announcement that the Nile would
overflow its banks within twenty days.

Nevertheless, the floods of the Nile were not always regu-
lated by Sirius, but by the sun when it melted the snow and the
rains falling in Ethiopia, where the highlands of the Blue Nile
were located. Thus, continuing to rely on the announcement
of the floods by the appearance of Sirius would have contin-
ued to lead to great catastrophes.

Thus, they resorted to a more precise element, such as the
pyramids, true albums of the ages...

Different studies with a single result

In his book *Cheops and the Great Pyramid*, Otto Heinrich
Muck wrote that due to a series of tragic floods during the
reign of Cheops, the 365.2536+ day stellar calendar had to be
changed for the 365.2422+ day solar calendar. Later an extra
day was added every four years in order to compensate for
the difference.

Likewise, Schwaller de Lubicz demonstrated in his
book *The Temple of Man* that the Egyptians did not use
either the astral year or the tropical solar year, but a Sothic
year which was based on the cycle of the fixed star Sirius.
Thus they reached the exact amount of 365.25 days. To this
archaeologist and philosopher, who was in Luxor for

twelve years measuring and studying its temples, tombs and hieroglyphics, the fact that the Egyptians managed to discover that Sirius is the only fixed star with an invariable cycle of 254.25 days shows that they must have spent a long time making painstaking observations, thanks to which they found the best way of capturing them.

According to the conclusions reached by Schwaller de Lubicz, we can deduce from the Egyptian texts that if Sirius' appearance had stopped being visible, it would not have prevented the priests from Heliopolis from continuing to make highly precise calculations. Once they knew this information, they communicated it to the other temples in Egypt. We have discovered that there was a difference of about four days in the heliacal appearance of the star among the observations made in Thebes and those in Memphis.

For his part, Muck emphasized that, in order to highlight the importance of the 1460 cycle, this figure was inscribed in the earth that surrounded the Great Pyramid. A cortege of priests, all dressed in white tunics, made a liturgical walk around the Pyramid, while they rhythmically chanted until completing the 1460 steps. These were subdivided into twenty-five inches, only to be divided once again into five.

Curiously, Muck's twenty-five inch step was the same length as Piazzi Smyth's sacred cubit, one hundred of which make the size of an English acre (0.4047 hectares).

The precession of the equinoxes

Schwaller de Lubicz reached the conclusion that in Egypt there was a Sothic calendar, as well as a civil calendar for marking the annual festivals, something he owed to the fact that he had learned to measure that phenomenon known as the 'precession of the equinoxes'.

If an observer located in the northern hemisphere wanted to have a simple image of the precession, they would have to stare toward the east. But they would have to do so just a moment before sunrise on the spring equinox, when dawn begins to brighten the eastern horizon. Then they would find the current astrological sign of Pisces. Nevertheless, in 2000

BC, this would have been Aries, and following a logical progression, in 400 AD it would have been Taurus, while in 2300 it will be Aquarius, a relationship that could be expanded upon using further examples.

It could be said that the entire zodiac was going backwards in relation to the dawning of the equinox, but at a very slow pace, one degree every seventy years and 30°, or one constellation, every 2,920 years.

It is believed that this precession of the equinoxes was discovered by Hipparchus in the second century. However, in different ancient writings on the zodiac, we can read: *The bull always signals the arrival of spring*. This must be considered the best proof that in the year 400 BC at least, astronomical observations related to the equinox were already being made.

However, the phenomenon of the precession was not understood by the scientific world until the brilliant Isaac Newton demonstrated it. He started from the fact that the Earth shifts as it rotates, leading to its celestial pole making a slow circle in the skies around the fixed pole of the solar system, which is the pole of the ecliptic. For any terrestrial observer who could see dawn on the equinox, this slow revolution would make the equinoxes happen twenty minutes earlier each year with regard to the zodiac constellations visible in the sky.

The ancient Egyptians, the initiates, must have had very precise means when calculating the slow pace of the precession of the equinoxes. According to Cotsworth, one of these wise men must have invented a structure which would allow him to form an exact stellar calendar. Through this calendar, he could have recorded the apparent movement of the stars in the sky. He obviously would have also had to find their orientation, using an exact meridian oriented in relation to a fixed point on the Earth.

In the mastaba of Pen-Meru which Reisner studied, there appears a hieroglyph that refers to the Great Pyramid as a solar temple. It was a monumental building with a platform on which a small pointed obelisk had been placed. That way, the problem of observing the summer solstice was resolved. On the top of a truncated pyramid an obelisk could be erected, placed at an exact height so that the edge of the platform could record the shortest shadow at twelve o'clock on the longest day of the year.

Cotsworth received a gift from Sir Gaston Maspero, the director of the department of antiquities at Cairo Museum. The gift was a curious hieroglyph which had not been deciphered, on which there appeared a drawing of a truncated pyramid which had a solar disk balanced on top. Cotsworth recognised the similarity between this figure and various European monuments and obelisks, especially the English and Scottish ones, which he himself had studied. After carefully examining them, he had to wonder:

How are they related to the Pyramid of Cheops?

A brief review of history

The way the ancient civilisations made their astronomical measurements always surprises modern scientists because of their precision. This is because the majority of them acted in accordance with a strictly rational methodology, without taking history into account, especially religious history.

The brilliant Isaac Newton began to work on the Theory of Universal Gravitation in the seventeenth century, but he had to wait about twenty years due to the simple fact that he could only make one measurement of the terrestrial meridian with a 10% inaccuracy. Meanwhile, in 200 BC, Eratosthenes was able to calculate the length of the meridian at 22,798 miles, with an error of less than 1%.

The scientists who criticised Davidson for claiming that the pyramids were repositories of information must have forgotten that in Babylonia, the daily movement of the Moon had already been calculated at 13° 10' and 35", an error of 1" according to the latest calculations... And this knowledge was acquired without making use of the powerful optical instruments available at the end of the twentieth century!

For the Egyptians, the year was composed of 365.2425 days, which made it coincide, as we have already seen, with the cycle of Sirius. This gives us the idea that they possessed great astronomical knowledge, for which they must have made use of powerful instruments, and not the simple 'mer-jet', or 'time observer' pole, which was a carved palm stick with a V-shaped opening on the upper part through which it is assumed that they found out the time at night by the height of the stars.

It is more logical to think that the Egyptians had a lens, as highly polished as the marble that covered the pyramids and with the increases needed for it to be used as a telescope.

Chapter XII

ASTRONOMICAL OBSERVATORIES IN EGYPT

A great astronomer

In his book *The Dawn of Astronomy*, the Englishman Norman Lockyer was the first to demonstrate a fact that was already obvious to many researchers: the ancient Egyptians used the pyramids as astronomical observatories. This great scientist's contribution was that he proved it using highly precise calculations, drawings that made it clear and provided conclusive evidence.

According to this astronomer, the Egyptian solar temples had been built so that, at dawn or sunset on the longest day of the year, the sun's rays penetrated a very long, ingeniously built corridor until reaching the centre of the temple. This light was controlled in turn by a series of pylons which served as screens in order for the beam to break the shadows and always fall on the same place.

To Lockyer, this brilliant skill could be clearly seen at Stonehenge, whose architectural complex had been precisely aligned in around the year 1680 BC. Thus it received the first light of the sun on the solstice, something that has recently been confirmed by the astronomer Gerald S. Hawkin, who used a computer for the calculations, as he told in his book "Stonehenge: Plans, Descriptions and Theories".

In these impressively beautiful Egyptian temples, the sun's rays were handled as water is when channelled, but with much greater precision and superior skill. They managed to make it cross two rows of minutely carved columns, just as the light of a star is channelled by ever narrower lenses in a telescope. Something similar was achieved with the light from the other celestial stars; they knew the best way to use them.

If a ray of sun penetrated about 1,476 feet into a narrow passageway until it reached a precisely oriented temple, it would only last a brief period of two minutes. First it would wax and then it would wane by gradually diminishing. Thus, the priests had to be very alert in order to record this phenomenon the precise moment it began. In this way, they could calculate the length of a year up to one minute or four tenthousandths, as we mentioned at the end of the last chapter.

Other very interesting details

On another visit to Egypt, Lockyer could see that Amon-Ra's Temple of the Sun near Karnak had been built in such a way that the sun's rays passed through the axis of the whole temple before reaching its sanctuary. But this only happened on the winter solstice, which was the longest day of the year. This was such an important piece of information that he characterised it this way:

I found myself before a high-precision scientific instrument, more sensitive than the instruments that I have used in England. I remain convinced that by this means, Egyptian astronomers could determine the length of the year with utter exactness.

He completed his study with an archaeological calculation which enabled him to deduce that the temple of Amon-Ra had been built in the year 3,700 BC. As Herodotus had written that in the temple of Tyre two columns of golden, green rock were raised that shone at midnight, Lockyer, explained it thus:

I have no doubt that in the middle of the darkness, the shine of the alpha star of Lyria, one of the brightest in the southern sky, sprang suddenly from the Egyptian temple. The light would have been so intense, especially when it traversed the clear air of Egypt, that it could provoke this apparent radiation in the columns, as Herodotus saw in the temple of Tyre.

These details make clear the wisdom of the Egyptian initiates, yet they do not make them magicians. However, if we add what Maspero tells us regarding certain 'tricks' used by the great priests, we do enter another highly interesting realm.

Even the smallest detail was planned

Maspero has written that the Egyptian magician-priests, the initiates, achieved that at a certain point in time, the jewels on the statues of the gods shone, sending blinding rays throughout the entire temple. This wonder could have been accomplished through various means, among them these two: the judicious use of the solar rays it was already receiving as a means of astronomical observation, which would have involved knowing the exact moment this short reception of light would take place; or magical power, which would enable them to convert a gem into a powerful source of light.

Since we have already explained the magician-priests' ease with making statues of the gods 'talk', we can add this other magical practice to the many that have been compiled throughout the centuries. But with regard to astronomy, we should highlight the fact that the Englishman Lockyer demonstrated that the temples oriented toward the Sun acted as calendars for thousands of years. We should take into account that the Earth's axis only moves one degree every seven thousand years, while the equinoxes change every three hundred years. The Egyptian architects had already planned for this phenomenon.

This change in direction is what is most surprising in the Egyptian temples – wrote Lockyer. *According to my observations through several years, I have been able to confirm that by modifying the orientation of some pylons, several patios and vestibules continue to preserve the same precision when making the calendar according to the Sun's rays.*

Since the earliest Egyptian wise men planned for any alteration up to the smallest detail, they took as their point of orientation the alpha star of the plough, but they also used Capella, Antares, Phact and the alpha star of Centaur. They did this when they used the temples as astronomical observatories and at the same time as repositories for their immense culture. Something very important must have taken place centuries later, as the ever-incisive Professor Lockyer tells us:

The great pyramids were built by an invading race, which brought new advances to astronomical science. Thus they used as their orientation the northern stars in the south, as well as other stars that appeared with total exactness in the east of the equinoxes.

Lockyer's theories were hotly debated by astronomers throughout the world, since they believed that they were too 'irregular' to adapt to historical facts. It is possible that this impeded the spread of the researcher's brilliant books, all of which were re-released in the 1970s. In addition, recent calculations made by computers have shown each of his theories and hypotheses to be correct.

The perfection of the Egyptian zodiac

Schwaller de Lubicz was one of the researchers who most based his work on Lockyer's theories, the majority of which he took pains to verify. Since his astronomical knowledge was equal to that of the English professor, he left us with a clear definition of the Egyptian zodiac:

This old zodiac measures 7 feet in diameter and is engraved in hard rock, such that it appears in relief. All the constellations are located in the shape of a spiral within which they move counter-clockwise, indicating the nocturnal route of the stars as seen from Earth. All the recognisable mythological figures, meaning the constellations near the pole, are these: a jackal for Ursa Minor, an ox foot for the Plough and a hippopotamus for the Dragon. Sirius is represented by a cow in a ship carrying a star between her horns.

Our north star is located in the centre of the circle. But the circle appears within a square, which was oriented to the walls of the temple, that is, about 17° to the east of due north.

138

The North Pole was also placed quite accurately over the constellation of the jackal or Ursa Minor, just as it appeared at the time the zodiac was engraved...

In accordance with current data, there is no doubt that the Egyptian astronomers knew about the existence of the two poles in the sky: a northern one that rotated around a fixed pole, which they called the "hole open to the sky". In addition they also knew that that this slow, constant circular movement caused the precession of the equinoxes.

An energetic defender of Egyptian science

Giorgio Santillano not only defended the idea that Egyptian science understood the precession, but he demonstrated it in many of his works. As a professor of history and philosophy of science at the Massachusetts Institute of Technology, he had great authority when raising ideas such as this:

At the moment when the solar temple was built with such exactness, we must understand that it required different reconstructions throughout about forty centuries, each time bringing with it a correction of its precise realignment in relation to a star... If we look at the Egyptian zodiac, in which the positions of the stars have been drawn with such accuracy as they were centuries ago, it is reasonable to assume that this civilisation knew about the precession of the equinoxes...

Since certain scientists continued obstinately refusing to accept that the Egyptians might have known about the precession of the equinoxes, since this discovery had been attributed to Hipparchus, Santillano did not vacillate when accusing them:

You are cultivating primitive ignorance of astronomical thought. I would go further: some of you do not know what the precession means.

The Egyptian initiates were convinced that the precession of the equinoxes was the fundamental mechanism of the universe, since in addition to regulating astronomical phenomena, it was responsible for all human and biological development. For this reason, since the beginning of history they moved the spring equinox from Taurus to Aries and later to

Pisces. This would be one-fourth of a complete cycle within the sky, which requires exceptional astronomical knowledge.

Santillano wanted to draw attention to Copernicus' system. To do so he emphasized that the precession was a consequence of the oscillation to which the Earth's axis is subject, a phenomenon that should not be viewed as mysterious:

In antiquity this phenomenon was endowed with a mysterious aura, just like any movement in the celestial sphere or the entire cosmos. Despite the fact that few people are capable of avoiding the excitement of astrology, we should take into account that the precession attained impressive characteristics. It ended up becoming a broad, unfathomable territory of destiny, as one and then another century went by while the invisible indicator of the equinox was slipping without anyone wanting to accept that it was. Only the Egyptians knew this and used it to identify all the astral rules and powers, in this way predicting their consequences on earth...

He had very solid scientific reasoning, proof that could not admit a single doubt and evidence that remains standing in the desert sands; nevertheless, there are still many people who refuse to accept that in many ways Egyptian civilisation surpassed ours of today. Perhaps because it ended up being violently defeated, conquered, to remain dormant throughout almost twenty centuries, while it was plundered, desecrated and damaged... Yet never erased from the face of the Earth!

We should still be amazed

But the astronomical knowledge was not only used by the Egyptians to make calendars or find out the distances between the Earth and the stars, since they also used it to obtain many geodesic and geographic data. This has been proven by Professor Stecchini, who has his doctorate in the sciences of classical measurement from Harvard.

Numerous ancient hieroglyphs show this, in papyrus, tablets and stone engravings. The Egyptian wise men could measure latitude with a margin of error of a few hundred cubits, which means a 'precision' that was not achieved until the eighteenth century AD. Thus they could measure

140

the circumference of the Earth, which we have already mentioned, and their entire country down to the smallest corner. They knew Egypt's exact co-ordinates, from the equator to the Mediterranean.

In order to achieve such precision they must have used means similar to modern telescopes and chronometers, something that in the Middle Ages during the time of the castles, not even the monasteries and cathedrals knew about unless it was written in the books, and it was certainly not practised.

To amaze us even further, we should add that the Egyptian wise men drew maps of the skies and earth they walked upon with an accuracy that the Portuguese navigators who reached India or Christopher Columbus himself would have desired. They also solved trigonometric problems... Did 'conservative' historians not write that they never got beyond addition?

More irrefutable proof

On the very thrones of many pharaohs a glyph was engraved in which can be found geodesic data that is a little difficult to interpret. Stecchini saw in it three figures referring to the Tropic of Cancer: a simple one of 24°, another more precise one of 25° 51', and another exact one of 24° 06'. All of them must have been used to get the Sun's shade during the summer solstice.

Another irrefutable piece of evidence that the Egyptians were great astronomers is found in the construction of the observatory on the island of Elephantine, near Syene. This place was chosen because it is located at 15' north of the current Tropic, which meant half the diameter of the Sun. They did this intentionally, because they knew that one can never look directly at the Sun but only at its outside edges.

When the Egyptians knew the real dimensions of their nation, they tried to simplify them. Thus they chose the Nile waterfalls and the edge of its delta, based on which they traced geodesic rectangles, which would be easier to remember.

Each of their cities and towns were also built based on the Tropic and the central meridian. These geodesic points were called 'stone navels' and were placed to represent the hemisphere north of the equator and the pole, always marked with meridians and parallels. For example, the 'stone navel' at Thebes is located in the main hall of the temple of Amon, precisely where the meridian and the parallel cross.

We should bear in mind that in order to attain this knowledge, it was necessary to have, which we do not tire of repeating, astronomical observatories of admirable accuracy. They also had to use a large number of men, greater than an army, in order to draw a totally straight meridian at 30° latitude, going from the Mediterranean to the equator, with a length greater than 1,864 miles, just as they marked another two equidistant lines located to the east and west in order to set the borders of Egypt.

A more primitive system of communication was used by the astronomers in order to establish contact when, for example, a star had reached its zenith. They lit a chain of torches like a type of lantern that reached the closest observatory which then passed the information on to the next one, which then passed it on to a third, and so forth in the cycle.

In his book "Ideal Metrology", H. G. Wood explains that the best astronomical observatories were the pyramids, as can be seen in one of these small monuments located in the Libyan Desert. By lighting a torch at night one can communicate from one pyramid to another, despite the fact that many of these monuments are veritable ruins.

The geodesic centre of the world

Egypt's astronomical and geographic knowledge was so admired by other nations that it became the geodesic centre of the world. Thus they did not hesitate to build their sanctuaries and capitals based on the Egyptian 'zero meridian', as done in cities as important as Susa and Persepolis, and even in the ancient Chinese capital, which was known by the name Anyang.

This custom became a tradition that was respected by the Greeks, Romans and Arabs until the Middle Ages. Later, other references were taken, due to the fact that the astronomical knowledge of ancient Egypt had reached Alexander the Great's Greece in fairly adulterated form, thus giving rise to a series of errors that it continues to suffer from today.

More on Egyptian astrology

All the inhabitants of Egypt believed that the pharaohs were gods and were thus in permanent communication with the cosmos and the spiritual powers. Thus, they took no important decisions without consulting the astrological priests, since the pharaohs delegated them their great powers.

However, as we have explained, these magician-priests were not charlatans. They were excellent astronomers, they had managed to draw such a precise zodiac that they could create astral maps and then make highly accurate predictions. They went even further, since they divided human beings into Martians, Jupiterians, Saturnians and Lunar inhabitants.

Many astrologers continue to preserve this classification in our times, just as they continue to use the days of the week, the names of the Sun, the Moon and the planets in accordance with Egyptian knowledge. Many of our holidays, such as Christmas and Easter, are based on the winter solstice and spring equinox which were imposed in the land of the pharaohs.

Sunspots

We know that the Egyptian initiates knew many of the effects caused by sunspots. In his book "The Scientific Basis of Astrology", Michel Gauquelin tells us some of these:

... These spots, which look like dark flowers on the surface of the Sun, develop powerfully and are extinguished. Throughout this phase, the Sun sends out gigantic clouds of incandescent gas, while fabulous magnetic storms are generated. While it spins on its axis, in a phase lasting twenty-seven days, the Sun aims these spots and volcanoes toward the 'target' of the

Earth. Thus, the number of waves and particles that fall on our planet increases. This turns human beings into inhabitants of the Sun's entrails...

... While orbiting, the Earth's position has a lot to do with the sunspots. For example, when Venus and the Earth are on the same side of the Sun, the effect caused by these spots is enhanced. There are earthquakes and the length of days is even modified. It is as if our planet's magnetic fields have gone crazy. Radio and television broadcasts become full of interference and other no less mysterious phenomena occur...

Scholars of the effects of sunspots have related them with number of icebergs floating in the Atlantic Ocean, the level of lakes, the concentric rings that appear in trees as they grow and the quality of French Burgundy wine. We could also give numerous other examples, such as those affecting the pelts of rabbits hunted on the American and Canadian borders.

Sunspots also modify cells, to the extreme degree that micro-organisms can unleash epidemics of epic proportions. Modern astronomers frequently cite the eleven-year solar cycles as the cause of many weather changes, especially when the atmosphere appears to have gone haywire.

Sunspots respond to the activity of the star-king who rules the Earth, as well as positive and negative ions. The former cause headaches and nausea in human beings, while the latter release optimism, relax the body and increase fertility.

Some of all these phenomena were known by the ancient Egyptians, as Proctor and other researchers have demonstrated. And they had sufficient means to anticipate them using the most advanced Astrology the world has ever seen.

They did not fear death

In his book on the Great Pyramid, William Kingsland was very vehement when demonstrating the knowledge the Egyptians had about human beings' relationship with the cosmos, or *with elements external to astronomy*, as well as when telling us that, in Egypt, it was believed that astrology formed part of the mysterious doctrine that united all human beings with the 'beyond'.

Death was never feared in the land of the pharaohs, even though they tried to reach it in the best condition possible. Thus, powerful men ordered their corpses to be mummified, and they asked to be surrounded by their most beloved objects once they passed the threshold of the 'beyond', their pets and their food. Sometimes they also wished to be accompanied by their wives.

To Egyptian initiates, the term 'millions of years' did not mean what it does to us, because they viewed it as something accessible. If death was a leap into the 'beyond', reaching this moment in reconciliation with the gods gave one the right to eternity, a belief that the Judeo-Christian and other religions did not hesitate to 'plagiarise'. Let us examine what Kingsland wrote on the beliefs of Egyptian worship:

This man's goal of initiation was to fully realize his divine nature, recover his spiritual powers through the best of his origins. Death was an exit from the material and physical life in order to enter into a state of perfection, harmony and knowledge identical to that possessed by a god...

Chapter XIII

THE GREAT POWER OF THE PYRAMID

Let us begin with an electrical experience

It might be considered impossible for a scientist as knowledgeable as Werner von Siemens, founder of the great German company that bears his name, to be tricked. It is known that, in 1859, while he was installing a telegraphic building in the Red Sea, he decided to climb to the top of a pyramid. While he scaled it quickly, the desert wind blew up a cloud of sand that almost blinded him.

Nevertheless, he managed to reach the apex. Since Siemens believed that he had performed quite a feat, he raised a finger in victory. Suddenly, an intense tickling sensation went through his finger, his hand, his arm and his whole body. He also heard a small crack. Despite the fact that the phenomenon seemed to him a small electrical shock, which he had experienced on other occasions, he was so impressed that he decided to make the experience complete.

He was perfectly aware of the experiment called the 'Leyden bottle'. He looked for a wine bottle with a metal neck, which he wrapped in wet paper. He climbed to the top of the pyramid once again and placed the bottle on top of his head... He could immediately tell that the bottle had become charged with static electricity! Then, taking due precautions, he made sparks fly when he touched it.

147

The power to desiccate and preserve

Even more surprising than this was what happened to the French blacksmith Antoine Bovis, who was a great fan of water divining (the practice of divining using a pendulum). While he was visiting the Chamber of the King in the Great Pyramid, he observed the corpses of cats and other small animals in its underground galleries, all of which were mummified, something that seemed quite strange to him since there the place was quite humid. Logically, none of these irrational beings belonged to the ancient Egyptian mummies.

Since Bovis was astounded, he decided to discover the cause of the mystery. Once he was back in Nice, his birthplace, he commissioned a carpenter to make him a wooden scaled reproduction of the Great Pyramid. When he had it, he tried placing it in a garden, orienting it toward the north and then placing a dead cat inside the pyramid. He was not too sure about the test although the matter made him uneasy. If he had been, he would never have done this.

The following week he decided to take out the feline corpse. What he found left him more amazed than when he found the animals in the galleries of the Great Pyramid: the body was mummified, did not smell bad and appeared dehydrated. Just like any good amateur researcher, he made other experiments with different animals, and with meat and bones as well. In all cases the result was the same: the material did not decompose, since the bodies and food were desiccated to the point of being mummified.

Since this great experiment was published in the newspapers at the time, a Czech radio technician called Karl Drbal repeated it, but with significant changes: the pyramid was made of cardboard and the elements to be mummified were beef and flowers. He also left a razor blade located at three-fourths of the floor (where Drbal imagined the Chamber of the King would be). The results were similar to those obtained by the Frenchman Bovis, with the addition that the razor blade became sharper, so much so that he was able to use it more than two hundred times.

Given these results he decided to patent the invention, thus putting onto the market a cardboard 'razor blade sharpener,

Pyramid of Cheops-style'. These are currently still being manufactured, but in polyethylene.

How many more things does the Pyramid do?

An American of Hungarian origin, Max Toth, bought the world rights to Drbal's patent. He marketed them very successfully, especially because he backed his claims by very interesting books, some of which have served as a source of inspiration for this book.

The pyramids made by Max Toth provide such convincing results, especially with Gillette brand razor blades made with normal steel, 'the blue ones', that they have become very successful. But this person went even further, since he was convinced that he could help any individual maintain a positive energy level in addition to obtaining many other benefits if he has the right pyramid.

A great many fortune-tellers who use wands in their sessions have seen that when they place these wands in the upper part of cardboard pyramids, they intersect the way two magnets would, a phenomenon that is repeated even if they are on different floors of the large building. Linda Goodman explains this in her book "Sun Signs" by the fact that small pyramids give off energy rays from their apex, which not only turn wands into magnets but that in special situations can make them spin around wildly.

The managers of the airline Swiss Air do not dispute the fact that the real pyramids, those built by the ancient Egyptians, are full of energy, especially since one of their planes lost control of its flight's instrument panel when flying over the Great Pyramid, without being able to explain the cause. Since then, they have ordered the route to be changed, and the problem that almost ended in tragedy has not occurred again.

We also have an explanation for these phenomena provided by L. Turenne, an engineer and former professor of radio: *All pyramidal shapes combine a series of different frequencies which act as emitters of cosmic energy.* Other researchers seek the reason why the Great Pyramid can operate as a lens of vast dimensions, capable of accumulating an incredible energy charge, due solely to its shape. They also mention its geographical location, its orientation, the angles formed by the triangles of its faces and the fact that it is not entirely solid.

This path leads us to Wilhelm Reich

For Worth Smith, the sarcophagus in the Chamber of the King has powers similar to the Hebrews' Arc of the Covenant. This is due to the fact that both have the same cubic capacity, in addition to having been designed to function as electrical generators. The power of both has been calculated, in this case by Maurice Denis-Papin, at 500 volts, able to reach 700 in special circumstances. The fact that people who are next to them are not electrocuted is due to the fact that they wore chaplets, which acted as insulators.

Along this path of examining the pyramids' powers, we find that the properties conferred on the Arc of the Covenant and the sarcophagus of the Chamber of the King closely resemble Wilhelm Reich's 'Energy Accumulator'. Reich was one of the most revolutionary sexologists in the mid-twentieth century, who postulated organic energy as the best way for human beings to achieve happiness.

When theories take on even greater proportions

We have already written that we respect even the most audacious theories, such as when they tell us that the ancient Egyptian scientists made the Great Pyramid a defensive device, since they had managed to capture the energy of Van Hallen's belts. Once received, they made it pass through an ionised path in the atmosphere itself through the use of a laser ray located at the apex of the pyramid.

However, these scientists were not able to handle so much power, and thus they committed an inexcusable error: when allowing such powerful energy to circulate, the concentration of it unleashed a cataclysm of such dimensions that it put the rotating axis of our planet off-kilter.

150

Another theory with many supporters is based on the truncated pyramid, or in one that intentionally did not have an apex. The Egyptians, who had attained all their great knowledge from 'men from outer space', were forced to create landing runways for the spaceships. They never knew when they were going to land until a few seconds before, always at night. Perhaps the communication was mental or reached them through the sun's rays and the other stars, which these 'astronomical observatories' used.

These were brief but highly profitable encounters among extra-terrestrials who knew the interior walkways of the pyramid, where they had to enter in order to establish contact with the high priests and other initiates. In this way they communicated the great secrets that have amazed the world; far from the inferior beings, who would have taken the 'men from outer space' as demons.

Curiously, Herodotus supports this theory in some way, since after visiting Babylonia he wrote the following:

In one of the city's highest towers I could see a very wide temple. Inside there was an enormous bed which appeared to be covered by very delicate spreads, which were surrounded by golden panels. I could not see a single statue near it, and I had been told that the place was only occupied at night by a local woman, the most beautiful, chosen by a god among all the virgins on Earth. The Chaldean priests confessed to me, whose truth I cannot determine, that at night this god came to this place in person in order to take possession of the beauty and later sleep until shortly before sunrise. Before the sun could discover him he had already gone away, leaving his lover very sad...

Does this story not resemble hundreds others relating a virgin being offered up to the gods, never to kill them, although always with a prize for the knowledge given by the divinity?

The great power of radon

A young Czech seer named Jan Merta, who currently lives in Canada, has written that red granite is a powerful radon emitter, a radio isotope. We already know that the Chamber of the King in the Great Pyramid was built using red granite.

According to Merta's theory, radon causes a decrease in the human aura. If we bear in mind that this protects the psyche and reduces the perceptions of the body's organs, we understand that a loss in the aura's power tends to increase extrasensory perception, which parapsychologists call ESP.

Merta has no doubts that the Egyptian initiates used radon. When one of them entered the sarcophagus, inside a place covered by red granite, his mental capacity, or ESP, reached such high levels that he could establish telepathic contact with superior beings in any place in the universe.

They could also make the intense electromagnetic fields, such as the Van Allen fields, be used to 'hide' the presence of an extraterrestrial visitor who might arrive on our planet. At the same time, it could interrupt the source of telepathic communication that had guided it.

The initiate could recover his spiritual powers inside the radon field while he was lying down inside the coffin. He also reached such a degree of freedom that he was in conditions to overcome the earth's force fields, such as gravity.

A pyramid for individual use

One of the divulgers of the individual use of this wonder is Annie Hasch, who explains the following in her book "The Power of the Pyramids":

... Building it oneself is the beginning of the art. One must preferably choose materials that are not conductors: wood, cardboard and plastic. But I advise you to begin with cardboard, because it is easier and cheaper. If it works, nothing shall stop you from building a more sophisticated one. Take four pieces of very hard cardboard, such as that used to reinforce large folders, a millimetre ruler, a pair of scissors and adhesive tape. The beginning consists of cutting four identical triangles, and joining them on their edges. The measures chosen are in relation to Cheops, but do not worry if they are off by a few inches. There is only one rule: the triangles have to be identical. Choose one of the pieces of cardboard and

draw a line 9.4 inches long width-wise. In the middle of this line, draw a perpendicular line that crosses the entire cardboard surface. Go back to the left side of the 9.4 inches and draw an oblique line that crosses the perpendicular line at 8.2 inches. Do the same on the other side. The meeting point of the two oblique lines and the perpendicular line will give shape to the third angle of the triangle and the pyramid's vertex. Repeat the same operation on the other three cardboard pieces.

But there is a much easier system. Cut the triangle from the first piece of cardboard and place it on top of the other three. Put the oblique lines against each other. Join them using adhesive tape. Find the central point and stand the whole thing up. Join the edges of the first and fourth triangle to form the pyramid. With a little more tape you will have a structure approximately 7.4 inches high which will be ready to carry out the experiments.

You can do this using a single piece of cardboard, as long as it is at least 7.4 inches wide and 20 high. Divide the lower width into two parts 48.8 inches long. The third will be 14.7 inches. Do the same in the upper part, but beginning with a 4.7 inches segment. All you will have to do then is join the edges of the segments of the lower and upper edges using diagonal lines in order to obtain four absolutely identical triangles. Cut the diagonal lines with a razor or scissors and assemble the pyramid as in the first case...

Advice for using the pyramid

The author herself recommends that the pyramids never be solid or full. They can be either opaque or transparent. She advises using cardboard instead of another material. For meditation, the ideal are pyramids with quite sharp edges, always empty and perfectly placed in a location free from any negative influences.

Before beginning to use the pyramid, it must be oriented; thus a compass is needed. Just place one side facing the magnetic north, never the geographical north. One must also have a notebook in order to note down the time, the day, the temperature in the place, the outside weather and the experience one wants to have. Another important piece of information useful to record is one's own mood, that is, the mood of the person who wishes to experience the benefits of the pyramid.

Since what is suggested has few tricks, one is encouraged to have a witness who must remain in the background without making comments until the experience is over.

Chapter XIV

JESUS, JOSEPH AND THE ESSENES

Jesus and the Pyramid

Many esoteric philosophers have written about Jesus' presence in Egypt, where he remained long enough to learn from the initiates. Paul Sedir writes the following passage in his book "Initiations":

Evening had fallen on the desert; meanwhile, the foreigners were nearing the pyramids. When night came, in the shadow of these impressive stone triangles the bonfires lit in front of the Bedouin tents acquired a reddish sheen that no one could ignore.

While the fathers spoke, young Jesus was playing behind a rock. He liked to draw lines in the sand using a stick. A little later, he called the eldest of the Bedouins and showed him his drawings, following the common impulse in children to show their works when they think they have done something extraordinary. However, as soon as the wise Bedouin saw what appeared in the sand, he was paralysed by shock.

He took some time to react. As soon as he did, he bent over to see the meaning of those exact lines, which consisted of geometric figures that did not allow for much doubt. It could clearly be seen since the light from a nearby bonfire reached there. The ancient Bedouin admired the exact replica, just like the best plans, of the Chambers of the King and Queen in the Great Pyramid. There also appeared the underground passageways, wells and other details known by very few.

The wise Bedouin turned to look at the young Jesus with great respect because he, just like all his nomadic desert people, knew the architectural secrets of the Great Pyramid. Since he had received the antediluvian inheritance, he knew that the pyramid, just like the sphinx, was one of the stone texts in which the initiates, the patriarchs, had kept all of the bases of their infinite wisdom. The pyramid's geodesic location, its orientation, its external and internal proportions, the angles made by its walls and hidden chambers and many other data showed the essential keys of astronomy, geography and sociology, of laws and politics, of philosophical and religious history. All of this had been captured in the geometric drawings traced by little Jesus in the sand...

The temptation to give credit to this story becomes such an irresistible impulse that it is worth following similar paths. What matters is for the imagination to play, to risk speculating and accepting that new things are never an abysm but a leap to what is possible within what has never before been imagined.

Jesus could be from Atlantis or...

We already know that in the prophecies enclosed in the Great Pyramid, many of the dates highlighted are related to Jesus: his birth, his mission as a prophet, his arrest, his crucifixion and his resurrection. But the most surprising is that he is not cited as a foreigner who would have access to all the secret knowledge of the initiates. This might be due to the fact that, as some researchers believe, Jesus never existed as the son of God, although he was a prophet.

Beyond the Christian texts, the general idea is that Jesus came to the Earth to leave a testimony of the perfection of human beings, of goodness brought to the level of sublime solidarity and the devotion of life for the planetary good. However, the real evidence that archaeology has found on Jesus' existence is quite scarce.

156

If we return to the esoteric writers, we can find fascinating theories which question the very existence of the Bible as a text of divine inspiration. It is more a compilation of the writings of a primitive solar religion whose members were forced to seek refuge in Egypt after Atlantis was destroyed. These were privileged beings that were able to escape before the great tragedy.

Imagining that Jesus might come from Atlantis or be a descendant of the few who managed to flee from that marvellous island-city, invites the mind to shoot off in all directions. And if we take for granted the fact that Christianity and Hinduism drew from the same source, we can image Jesus learning in Egypt and then in India and other places in Asia. The Evangelists themselves give us this possibility, since they leave an enormous gap of years between the young Jesus who argues in the temple with the wise scribes, and the adult Jesus who submitted to forty days of harsh trials in the desert.

"Your mind is not a tangled skein..."

We shall let Gerald Massy take us by the hand, but always keeping in mind this principle: *your mind is not a tangled skein, but a series of threads ready to follow the most unsuspected paths*. This author of a great controversial work tells us that about one hundred years before Jesus' birth there already existed two powerful solar religions. One of them called its god 'Hesus', while the other called him 'Kristos'. Since they never agreed, in Constantine's time there were tales of confrontation between their followers which imperilled the existence of the Roman Empire.

This threat required the Nicean Council be called in the province of Bithynia, which was a city located in Asia Minor. There, almost two thousand priests converged, but they did not reach an agreement on the way of ending their disputes. When it was proposed that they unify under the name of 'Hesus Kristos', only four hundred voted in favour, a minority that prevailed, since Constantine made sure to throw the most vociferous dissident out of the city.

From this historical moment onward, Massey tells us that Constantinople was created to become a Christian city. Since after some time it was understood that a leader had to be found, similar to the Hebrew, Moses, they chose the new-born son of a noble family since he would not be stained by any crime or sin. In this way, Apollonius of Tyana appeared, who was raised with the most liberal ideas, both in the sciences and philosophy. He was also allowed to study all the existing religions of the time, for which he had to travel throughout Asia and reach Egypt, where he received the majority of his knowledge. His knowledge was so great that he could predict the future, revive the dead and perform miracles.

Gerald Massey defends the existence of Apollonius of Tyana based on the fact that the archaeological proof that might demonstrate it is as scarce as that supporting the fact that Jesus was a real person. Nevertheless, what truly matters to us is that both passed through Egypt, learned from the initiates and then faced a highly similar destiny.

Joseph in Egypt

The Egyptian writer Ahmed Osman wrote the suggestive book "Strangers in the Valley of the Kings", in which his central character is Joseph, the Hebrew patriarch who led the tribe of Israel to Egypt. The most well-known story about this biblical character is that when he was seventeen years old he was sold by his jealous step-brothers to slave traders. In this way, he was led to the land of the pharaohs, where he entered into the service of a wealthy family. Since he made wise interpretations of the plagues of abundance and hunger that would fall on those lands, he was named Viceroy. Then, since Joseph was not bitter, he bade all his family to come to live at his side.

It is assumed that these events took place in the year 1569 BC. It is also known that the Hebrews fell into disfavour long after Joseph's death, leading them to live worse than slaves, a situation they escaped from thanks to having a leader like Moses.

The traditional story goes this far, but Ahmed Osman does not accept it. Since he has conducted his own research, he believes that Joseph was named Viceroy by the pharaoh Tuthmosis IV; who was succeeded by his son Amenophis III. Given the fact that in Egypt it was believed that their monarchs, as well as their families, were related to the gods, siblings married in order to not lose an iota of divinity. It was obligatory to start with the eldest daughter, who would marry the eldest son.

However, taking Osman's writing as a point of reference, Amenophis broke the tradition since he married Joseph's beautiful daughter, making her the Great Royal Wife. This forces us to believe the fact that Joseph was the grandfather of Eknaton and great grandfather of Tutankhamen. Since all these pharaohs died quite young, Tutankhamen's successor might have been Eye, Joseph's second son.

Interesting speculations

Through the Bible, we know that in one of the years of famine Joseph's step-brothers reached Egypt to buy wheat. They were attended on by Joseph, who hid his identity; however, he did not do so the second time they met. Since he was a good man, he told them: "You did not send me here but God; and he has made me father of the pharaoh..." This last sentence led Osman to make some interesting speculations:

Father of the pharaoh! I still cannot believe that we have read these words so frequently without giving them their rightful importance.

There was no doubt that this was a title. But, in what sense could Joseph be considered father of the pharaoh? He himself, regardless of his age, had a father from his people. It also seemed possible that Joseph was referring to an allegorical title derived from his prominent position as Viceroy, if we consider, for example, that Tutankhamen, who was under nineteen years of age, had a Viceroy who was eighty and called, despite the difference in age, 'son of the King of Kush'. My instinctive reaction was to think that the words meant exactly what they claimed, and my thoughts turned

*immediately to Yuya. From the time of the Hyksos kings until
the New Empire that followed it, Yuya is the only person, as
far as we know, who in Egyptian history holds the title of
'father of the pharaoh'. Nevertheless, it is obvious that Yuya
did not have royal blood, since his mummy was found at the
beginning of the century in the Valley of the Kings in a tomb
located between those of two pharaohs. Would this person
and Joseph be one and the same – apparent – foreigner in the
Valley of the Kings?*

Ahmed Osman's speculations led him to conduct a
lengthy investigation with no intention of offending supporters of the Bible and the Koran. He was convinced deep down
that if his ideas were correct he could create a point of union
between the Hebrew and Islamic religions.

Yuya's tomb

Osman devoted himself to studying all the books written
on the matter, since he knew various oriental languages, was
living in London, and was a writer and journalist. One of his
points of reference was when Yuya's tomb was found, in 1905,
precisely in the same place where the mummies of Ramses III
and Ramses XI had been located. The last phases of excavation were being overseen by Arthur Weigall, Theodore M.
Davis and Gaston Maspero, the general director of the Cairo
Museum. Thanks to the second, we know what happened:

*... We tried to put the candles together, but they gave off
so little light that our vision was blurry, so we only captured
the glint of gold. But after a time I managed to distinguish a
long funerary sled on which the deceased's coffins and
mummy were usually laid to place them inside the tomb. It
measured about 78 inches and was made of wood covered
with bitumen from Judea, as shiny as the day it was
anointed. In its upper part, the coffin was decorated by a
gold leaf trim about 6 inches wide with engraved hieroglyphics. When I pointed this out to Mr Maspero, he gave me
the candle immediately and, along with mine he approached
the inscription in order to read it. He immediately said
'Iouiya'. Logically excited by the announcement and blinded*

by the light of the candles, I unintentionally approached the sarcophagus, leading Mr Maspero to shout at me: "Careful!" I moved my hands away and could see that if the candles had touched the bitumen, which was about to happen, the sarcophagus would have caught fire, something that would have prevented us from making important discoveries...

After this small incident, they could see the enormous amount of valuable objects scattered throughout the tomb. This led them to install electricity, which allowed them to locate a second coffin, which corresponded to Tjuyu, Yuya's wife. However, the proof that a pyramid thief had arrived, perhaps many centuries earlier, somewhat discouraged the researchers.

Fortunately, the mummies were intact, as were the inscriptions which allowed them to learn about the enormous number of titles that Yuya had received in his life. When his mummy was unwrapped, they could see *that he seemed to be a person of dominant appearance, with a strong character and a noble face; he could be described as a tall man with fine white hair, a large hooked nose similar to that of a Syrian, thick, sensual lips and a prominent, wilful chin; he appeared to be a cleric, since there was something in his mouth that resembled Pope Leon XIII; and noting his well-preserved features it could be assumed that he was the initiator of a powerful religious movement that his daughter and grandson completed.*

The author of this last comment, Arthur Weigall, was referring to Tiye, Yuya and Tjuyu's daughter, whom Amenophis III married and made the Great Royal Wife, and their son Amenophis IV (Eknaton). They closed the temples, destroyed the traditional gods and instated monotheism, taking the God of Israel as their reference, new data that encouraged Ahmed Osman to continue his research.

Joseph and Yuya were the same person

Perhaps the best evidence that the Hebrew patriarch Joseph and the pharaoh Yuya were the same person comes from chronology. The former lived between the years 1453 and 1378, while the latter also lived in a similar period, despite the fact that dates are not very precise in the Bible. But it does mention many deeds, which coincide with those of Yuya.

To Ahmed Osman, the evidence found admits no doubt: Joseph and Yuya are one and the same. It is true that he did not prove so categorical, since he wrote an almost two hundred page book to demonstrate it, a very pleasant text, almost like a police investigation, which we recommend to all aficionados of Egyptology.

The origin of the Essenes

The word Jehovah comes from the word 'Yanohaw', which when written in ancient Hebrew becomes 'Yhwh'. We should especially remember that the Israelites were forbidden from writing or uttering this holy name and so had to resort to substitutes such as 'Elohim' or 'Adonai'. To the Israelites, 'Yhwh' was the divinity of war and because of his essence he was the principle god, although not the only one. When they used the term 'Lord of the Armies', they were referring to one god within a group of gods, because they were polytheists and not monotheists.

Among the writings found on the Dead Sea, various mentioned the Qumran sect, which had much to do with the Essenes. It also appears to offer many of the messages that hundreds of years later the Christian religion would call their own. Precisely in the year 200 BC, in the lands we now call the Middle East, various religious sects with very different doctrines were found. However, among all if them, this one stands out for its holiness and desire for solitude.

The Essenes did not live anywhere, but they could be found everywhere. Their condition as travellers allowed them to transmit their message from one place to another. They had no property and only carried what they needed to survive, and everything they obtained was deposited in a common fund which was used so that other members could cover their basic needs. Their main objective was to help the poor and the neediest. As the ancient Egyptians had done, these great altruists worshiped the Sun, kneeling during the first minutes of dawn to dedicate their prayers to it.

The Essenes saw themselves among Nature, dressed in white robes and only bathing in cold water, which they saw as the best way of purifying themselves. During the summer, they preferred to find mountain streams and springs made by the melting snow instead of the lukewarm pools of the rivers that crossed the plains and valleys. Since they were aware that they were human beings full of weaknesses, they sought the help of the angels. Each Essene had their own, but they swore never to reveal their name.

The Essenes' rites were few, perhaps because they believed that every person was a 'living temple'. In order for them to defend themselves against the threats that appeared before them on the roads they travelled on their constant journeys. Nonetheless, when several of them were together, they tried to form groups of twelve, along with a priest, in order to eat around a table. The food was as simple as could be, although there was always bread and wine for the priest to bless by extending his hands over them before beginning the collation. For the Essenes, there existed a Master of Virtue, and they awaited the coming of a prophet or messiah...

Having reached this point, we have a most opportune question: *are there not a great many similarities between the Essenes and Christians?* This coincidence led Massey to go even further, since he puts forth the hypothesis that Christianity took so many things from the Essenes in order not to scare the people during that age. Since they had seen that the Essenes were admired and loved, presenting a "different doctrine, but one that resembled the other" must have worked very well.

Let us turn once again to Jesus

To Massey, the word 'Christ' does not refer to a divine name, to the son of God, but to a position, similar to the word 'the anointed one', which in ancient times referred to a priest or a King in order to indicate that they were a prophet and a

163

messiah. In the gospel, it rarely says that Christ or Jesus was God.

Archaeologists and religious scholars agree that it is very difficult to prove the existence of Nazareth, which was where Jesus was supposedly born. Nor have they been able to demonstrate, with on site excavations or by reviewing the writings remaining from the time, that the 'murder of the innocents' took place.

With regard to the term 'Redeemer of Humanity', attributed to Jesus, there are enough hieroglyphs to know that the Egyptian god Osiris had earned this name thousands of years earlier. And the beginning of the metric calendar, which is based on the winter solstice, called 'the date of the Conquering Sun', was chosen by Christians to be Jesus' birth date.

Chapter XV

THE PRESERVATION OF LIFE

The truth continues to stand tall

Many have pillaged the Pyramids, and much damage has been caused to their structure and insides, but they remain standing on the land of the Nile valley. No other ancient civilisation has left such valuable testimony of its existence, all of it extraordinary, ready to be interpreted in one way or another. But what no one can question is their beauty, how impressive their forms are and the message of mystery that each of them conveys.

There are numerous historians who understand that the treasure of the ancient Egyptians can never be seen in the fact that they accumulated gold, silver or precious stones inside their pyramids and temples. The true treasure is found in the quality of their goldsmith craftsmanship, their paintings, the delicacy with which they treated wood, marble and other materials, in the mummies and many other wonders. No one can dispute the fact that Velazquez's "Las Meninas" or Michelangelo's "Pieta" are invaluable, because they constitute a symbol of sublime perfection in art. Then, what could we say about any of the finds from the pyramids?

The historian Kurt Lange left us impressive testimony in his book "Pyramiden, Sphinxe, Pharaonen":

... In January of 1929, the expedition sponsored by the

Metropolitan Museum of New York, led by Winlock, was uncovering the northern exterior of the wall of the temple at Der-el-Bahri as far as the adjacent rocks. They suddenly discovered one of those small wells, hidden by rocks and debris, which generally lead to royal burial grounds. They decided to excavate the well and after 49 feet they found a narrow passageway which formed a right angle and lasted another 19 feet until it reached a deep pit, which seemed to be used as a trap or obstacle. It took them several hours to cross this abysm. The effort was worth it, since they continued through various burial chambers, in the last of which they found an immense sarcophagus in the shape of a woman.

It was, in truth, a magnificent work approximately 9.8 feet long, cut in the most dazzling Syrian cedar, which must have originally been covered in gold leaf. The innumerable furrows in the head represented the hair of the deceased woman, and the scales on a part of the covering stood out thanks to a bluish paste. The researchers thought that in a later restoration cheaper material had replaced the original material, which surely was of incalculable value... For whom was the sarcophagus and who had restored it?

The funerary inscription answered the first of these questions, saying that there rested no one other than the princess Meryamon, daughter of the great Tuthmosis III and wife of Amenophis III. Her face framed by the exuberant wig was one of the most noble and distinguished of those that have reached us from ancient Egypt.

The sculpted head on the sarcophagus had preserved a surprising lifelike resemblance throughout the millennia. Around the nose, the mouth and the chin a combination of secret haughtiness and resignation were insinuated, which highlighted her real feminine charm. The eyes made from obsidian and threaded in bronze conferred an expression of melancholic serenity on her features.

Despite the fact that hundreds have been found, most of them beautiful, no other female portrait from ancient Egypt impressed the investigators as much as this one. Her arms, crossed over her chest, held papyrus sceptres: symbols of the queen and god, which like magical amulets meant eternal youth, permanent freshness, greenness and fertility.

166

The answer to the second question was provided by the bandages that enveloped the mummy. Indeed, by the inscription they contained it was discovered that the tomb had been restored in the year 1049 BC by express mandate of King Paynozem, since when he found out that it had been desecrated and pillaged, he temporarily repaired it once again and walled in the tomb...

With this in-depth description we have been able to discover a work of art, a cultural treasure, one more among the thousands left by the Egypt of the Pyramids. We have also obtained proof that back then there were already plunderers, despite the many obstacles and traps installed in the underground galleries, all of which should have been secret. But it is possible that the perpetrators were the very workers who built the galleries, since the legends that they were killed so that they would not reveal the great secret are not true.

The preservation of life

On the 22nd January, 1938, in excavations being carried out in Saqqara, W. B. Emery and his associates made one of those discoveries that are capable of making the imagination soar heavenward.

When they opened the tomb of an important person from the 2nd dynasty from the year 2700 BC, they found the funerary offerings in the most perfect state of preservation... And it was food served on baked clay plates and bowls, all of it with the appearance of being edible right away, except for the fact that it was cold and gave off no odour!

The researchers could not believe it. Nonetheless, reality was staring them in the face. There were roasted skewers of meat, fish with sauce, legumes boiled with herbs and spices, ripe fruit, cookies that appeared to be recently baked, small circular and triangular buns that appeared to still be soft, and even beef cutlets surrounded by a thick condiment.

Once the excitement of the find was overcome, from the impact from one of the most surprising discoveries, the scientists saw that some of the food was not the same size as if it were served when cooked, since it had shrunk a bit, and

167

some of the plates and bowls seemed to be cracked. Another proof of the find's antiquity was the type of condiments, which did not correspond in any way to those of modern-day Egypt, which they had all suffered from until adapting to it. Emery commented with a smile that they might have been the butt of a joke, leaving the tomb full of food. But the proper archaeological examination certified that the remains found were more than 3,000 years old.

This leads us to recall that in March, 1963, biologists from the University of Oklahoma confirmed that the skin cells of Princess Mene, or her mummy, were in such a state to be able to 'come back to life', as if in some mysterious way, through an extraordinary preservation technique, her skin had been dormant.

When this news was published, many commentators compared it to hibernation. But the mummy lacked her vital organs: brain, heart, lungs, etc. At the beginning of the 1960s, organ transplants were almost science fiction, which is not true at the end of the twentieth century.

Why should we stop ourselves from imagining that Princess Mene's mummy was awaiting fabulous surgeons, who perhaps came from outer space, to put into her body all the organs she was missing, as well as blood or another similar product, in order to bring her back to life?

With regard to the food found in the tomb at Saqqara, we can also play with assumptions. If food, flowers and other elements can be preserved in a pyramid made of cardboard, as long as its measurements follow the scale of the Great Pyramid and it is oriented toward the polar north, why can we not believe that this Egyptian banquet was preserved throughout more than three thousand years by the fabulous effects provided by the real pyramid?

Four million sarcophagi!

The Egypt of infinite surprises reaches the limits of the incommensurable when the love they had for their innumerable holy animals is studied. We have written that nothing seemed unworthy, specially outside bad human actions, because they were convinced that even the most insignificant blade of glass or mote of dust was the work of the gods. Nothing could be considered inferior, especially if it had been named by the voice of the gods.

Doctor Sami Gabra made another great discovery (how many have deserved this description in this book?), when he found what he called 'the city of the holy animals'. It was a type of gigantic temple in which the mummies of animals such as cats, monkeys, ibises, baboons, crocodiles and many other animals had been kept. Remains of palm trees and other tropical trees were found, as if they were waiting for some of the animals that live in them to come back to life in order to use them again.

Before reaching this secret place of immense size, Doctor Gabra had to descend a staircase with about 120 steps. At the end of it he found a room in which the tables and many of the tools used for embalming were still preserved, as were the stone vats containing remnants of ointments, some of which still had the penetrating odour of resin.

At this point we shall let Kurt Lange continue with the description of the scene and the gifts it provided:

When one descends to the underground galleries that must have been dug by the contemporaries of Tuthmosis and Amenophis and then incessantly enlarged, one runs the risk of losing oneself in that maze of dark corridors that crisscross and eventually reach 393 feet in length. The walls are full of niches made to hold the animals' sarcophagi, reminiscent of the 'loculi' of the catacombs. These are also catacombs, and they show the imprint of the people who built them throughout various centuries.

When this shadowy world, whose emptiness and judicious layout would not have been unworthy of those of Hercules, was discovered, it was literally crammed with amphorae, all of them with their corresponding ibis mummies. No fewer than four million of these sarcophagi have been extracted from there for investigation! It is impossible in this part of the world to find another so highly populated necropolis. In the still-unexplored crypts of this dark labyrinth there must be many of them. In one of the corridors, there still exist the altars devoted to the god Thot by Ptolemy and Alexander IV,

169

the unfortunate son of Alexander the Great and the beautiful Asian prince, Rojana.

Suddenly the visitor's heart stops when he unexpectedly finds himself face to face with a gigantic baboon, which stares at him from an altar illuminated with an invisible reflector. Large wooden ibises appear to guard that mysterious door which Sami Sandra penetrated in the only human tomb in that immense animal necropolis: that of the great priest Ankh-hor.

This is the best evidence that the Egyptians were not only great mathematicians, geometricians, magicians, philosophers and wise men in all the other material and spiritual disciplines, since they scrimped on neither cost nor art when preserving the mummies of all their sacred animals.

Many animals were treated like gods

The best of the ancient writers, the immortal Herodotus, tells us the following about the Egyptians' relationship with animals:

...Despite the fact that it borders on Libya, Egypt cannot be considered a country with many animals; however, those that live among them, regardless of whether they are domesticated or wild, become considered holy. If I dared to express the origins of this worship I would risk entering the terrain of the gods, something from which I try to escape from unless forced to do so.

The treatment of animals follows these rules: each of them has its caretakers among the men and women of Egypt. This worthy role is inherited by sons from their fathers. The inhabitants of the cities make their offerings in the following way: those who venerate the divinity to which the animal is consecrated totally shave a child's head or leave it half or one-third shaved, because it is ordered that the weight of this hair in silver be placed into the hands of the servants that take care of the family's holy animal. This silver must provide enough money to purchase the fish or other food to be served to the animal.

If someone should voluntarily take the life of one of these animals, he would immediately be accused of capital punish-

ment; but if he did so involuntarily, he would be forced to pay the fine stipulated by the priests. However, if the animal were an ibis or a falcon, even if the death were caused by carelessness, there would be no mercy for the perpetrator, since he would be immediately executed...

...When fires begin, cats' behaviour is astounding, because people prefer to save them before dousing the flames. But these animals end up escaping, leaping over the heads or bodies of their protectors in order to flee the fire. If something like this happens, the people of Egypt feel sad and desolate. If a cat dies in a household, even due to old age or an incurable illness, its owners and servants shave their eyebrows; but if a dog dies, they also shave their entire heads and bodies. Sacred animals are led to a special temple to be embalmed and are then buried in a place called Bubastis...

... In certain places in Egypt, crocodiles are adored, while in others they are considered mortal enemies and are thus hunted to the death, something not done by the people of Thebes and the cities located on the shores of Lake Moris, since they consider them sacred animals. In these two places they even train crocodiles and are able to touch them while they are being fed. Crystal and gold rings and bracelets with precious stones are placed on the forearms of some of these animals. The laws stipulate the food that must be served to crocodiles as well as the treatment they must receive, which I consider to be superior. When they die, they are embalmed and then kept in coffins that are considered sacred...

Has there existed any civilisation in the world capable of treating animals in this way? Certainly some people recall the case of some dog, cat or other lucky pet, whose capricious owners left an inheritance of millions of dollars, pounds or francs; however, these are isolated cases never involving an entire species. Caligula, too, named his horse 'Caesar' in a fit of madness.

The Egyptians' behaviour with animals gives us the idea of an exquisite civilisation, very rich in every sense, which since it had its material and spiritual needs covered, could completely devote itself to animals... and men... sublimely!

171

The extraordinary hypothesis of 'Heb-Sed'

Within this chapter devoted to the preservation of life in many aspects, it might be interesting to review some characteristics of the funeral rites. It is known that in many cases what was most sought was the resurrection of the pharaohs. As G. Reisner has demonstrated in the pyramids of Meroe (in Abyssinia or Ethiopia) the monarchs of these tribes were buried along with their subjects.

Many scenarios have been described with regard to the provision that a pharaoh or king could never govern more than thirty years. After this time he was encouraged to 'put himself to death in the company of his ministers, his families and his greatest allies'. If he refused to obey these norms, which were considered holy, the high priests and military officers had to be charged with executing this large group of formerly important people. The archaeologist, Fakhry, wrote the following on this subject:

In many of these tribes, a chief had the possibility of renewing his youth through rituals and sacrifices, with the sole purpose of lengthening his reign. At the beginning of history, the Egyptians most likely practised these regicides; however, the pharaohs' ritualised death had ended by the first dynasty. The chiefs practised the Festivals of Sed (Heb-Sed) as the best means of renewing the power of their youth and prolong their reign. The practice of 'Heb-Sed' continued until the end of Ancient Egypt. There are many relief representations of these ceremonies on the temple and tomb walls...

The most complete of these representations is found in the complex of Djoser in Saqqara, where there is a large number of buildings that make up what has been called the 'courtyard of Heb-Sed'. The great importance conferred on this festival can be seen in the fact that it lasted such a long time; thus the entire architectural complex is dedicated to it. In some later pyramids, such as that of Sahure from the fifth dynasty, there are also representations of 'Heb-Sed'.

An explanation for the empty tombs

The importance in Egypt of the festival of 'Heb-Sed' can be seen in the buildings dedicated to Djoser, whose majesty and sober elegance prove artistic levels that were not equalled even by the architects of the Acropolis in Athens. The restoration work for the 'Service des Antiquetés de l'Egypte' led by the architect J. P. Lauer has enabled us to admire nowadays an architectural work that was created perfectly at the dawn of human culture.

There is no doubt that the festivals related to 'Heb-Sed' were linked by magical ceremonies that have not yet been explained. This does not prevent it from being possible to guess at their importance, since we have the monuments to Djoser or Cheops built to be more than just mementoes of a pharaoh. We have already explained the multiple functions that the pyramids performed. We shall add the desire to prolong the reigns, to be reincarnated.

It is perfectly believable that the 'Heb-Sed' ceremonies were a representation of the pharaoh's death and rebirth if we bear in mind the enormous number of empty tombs found in the pyramids and temples. They were not plundered, rather they were waiting for the king to be reincarnated. Thus, Manetho wrote: *Cheops ascended to the sky in body and soul.*

In antiquity, this was understood as the mummy not being in the pyramid, an idea we can support with prayers from the "Book of the Dead":

Raise up, oh King Unas! Raise your head and shake off the earth from your body! ...From now on you shall not sleep in your tomb so that your bones do not decompose. Your ailments have disappeared and you are already on your way to heaven...

Another theory on the empty tombs lies in the fact that some pharaohs built the inside of the pyramids, especially the Chamber of the King, before the entire complex. This explains why in many Egyptian sepulchres we can see that the coffins are larger than the doors, without assuming that the carpenters and other artists assembled them piece by piece inside, since this was not customary practice.

Chapter XVI

WHEN OUR IMAGINATION SOARS

Egypt was evil

We shall now take a gratuitous leap through time; in due time you shall see where we intend to land. In the Middle Ages, superstition covered the pyramids with a veil of evil. It was told that these buildings were the refuge of ghosts, evil spirits and vermin. One Arab legend warned that a cruel naked woman wandered through the Great Pyramid, whose chant fascinated anyone who approached the old stones to the point of madness such that he would inevitably turn himself over to the insatiable appetite of this seductive harpy.

Some of the great visitors who reached the Nile valley wrote atrocities on *those horrible stone barriers, which are not even useful for stopping the permanent advance of the desert sand*. After travelling the area where the pyramids lie, the rabbi Benjamin ben Jonah from Navarra exclaimed:

These ugly triangle-faced castles were built by magical art!

Curiously, when we listen to the incendiary words of Abd-al-Latif, who was the master of medicine and history in Baghdad, he decided to enter one of the few pyramids that had a door forced open. He did so to see if it was true about the enchantment: however, he had to leave quickly after a few minutes. He was terrified, short of breath and covered with sweat. As soon as he recovered, thanks to the help of some of his students, he had to explain, with his head hanging low:

I am ashamed of my own weakness; but I felt so frightened that I almost fainted, especially when I was attacked by so many bats and other repulsive beasts... Promise me you shall never repeat my experience! Because I have receive fair punishment for my rashness!

We believe they heeded his warning, since the pyramids' infamy did not disappear. Many people contributed to it, such as the Englishman, John Mandeville, when he wrote a book entitled "The Travels of Sir John Mandeville", in which he attempted to visit Egypt with the idea of exploring the pyramids, but could not enter any of them because they were full of poisonous snakes. Later it was proven that he had not even left his country, and everything told in his work was pure fiction.

A glimmer of hope

With the arrival of the Renaissance, culture resurged. Just as painters and sculptors were freed from the imposition of religious motifs in order to look back at ancient Greece and the Rome of the Caesars, they also raised their sights toward Egypt. But they only knew its mythology, a little of its history and nothing more, all of it told by Herodotus and other authors, the majority of them extremely ancient.

A similar interest might have motivated John Greaves, a mathematician and astronomer who had studied at Oxford and taught geometry in London. He left England in 1638, when Magellan had already circumnavigated the world (a journey that was completed by Juan Sebastian Elcano) and seemed to have closed the cycle of the great maritime discoveries and explorations, impressive accomplishments that were crowned by poor geographic and astronomic knowledge.

It is known that Greaves wanted to find information in the Great Pyramid that would allow him to measure the circumference of the Earth. First he reached Italy, where he might have established contact with the wise Girolamo Cardano, a Milanese physicist and mathematician who admired Leonardo da Vinci. Thus the Englishman found out that many intellectuals were convinced that beyond the Greeks a civilisation that knew the exact sciences with greater precision must have existed. They based this on the simple fact of the pyramids' architecture, and their reasoning went something like this:

If an architect today is forced to resort to innumerable measurements and calculations before beginning to build a humble church, what would the Egyptian architects have needed in order to build those fabulous stone cathedrals they raised on the banks of the Nile?

Greaves began by measuring some of the most famous Italian buildings. However, it was in the Vatican gardens where he found an element that would become key to his research. On the statue of a young architect from the first century AD named T. Statilius Vol Aper, he saw his professional instruments and, most importantly, a Roman foot.

Thanks to this, he could carry out measurements, comparing them with the English foot. Later he would do the same with the Greek foot. In this way he approached the basic measurement chosen by the architects in ancient Egypt. He also commissioned instruments, some of his own design, to be manufactured in order to measure the pyramids. Securing funds for the trip was a little complicated, but he ended up with all the money he needed thanks to the Archbishop of Canterbury.

Once he was in the Nile valley, he enthusiastically began to climb the pyramids to begin the first measurements. However, when he decided to enter a descending gallery, there were so many bats flying around him that he had to shoot his guns thinking that they were going to kill him. The din of the gunpowder was so deafening, with all its echoes, that Greaves was dazed and almost suffered a fatal accident.

This lesson made him more cautious. Since he had good helpers at his service, they showed him the paths followed by Al-Mamun. After taking out a great deal of granite and limestone remnants, as well as tonnes of debris, the English researcher was able to enter the galleries. Many were invaded by the bats, but he had various means of frightening them to prevent them from causing further harm. Another obstacle to be overcome was the bat excrement and pieces of marble and other materials left by Al-Mamun's servants when they destroyed walls after finding there was no treasure there. All of this meant more delays, though these did not discourage him.

Science backed by logic

Greaves went through the corridors opened by Al-Mamun's servants, but he could go no further. This led him to think that it was incredible that the entire fabulous architectural complex was only used to keep an empty sarcophagus. He imagined that it must have been used for some other purpose, but he did not dare to make hypotheses without having minimum scientific elements.

The measurements he made at the base of the Great Pyramid came to 693 feet; but he committed an error when he added 70 because of the enormous stones that he could not remove. He was more precise in measuring the ashlars, which are 207 and the total height of the complex: 499 feet.

His opinion on Cheops' pyramid can be summarised by these sentences: *It is a highly majestic work of art, not one that is inferior, in terms of artistic interest and the wealth of its materials, compared to the most sumptuous and magnificent buildings that we have in the West. It was built with ashlars of polished limestone, cut identically in squares or tablets of great dimensions. In addition, the fineness and articulation of all the joints is so exact that they can hardly be distinguished from one another at first glance.*

Upon his return to England, Greaves was named Savilian professor of astronomy at Oxford as a reward for his work exploring the Great Pyramid. He included his calculations and other data in a small academic book entitled "Pyramidographia", which unleashed an impassioned controversy. Thus the flame that would remain burning for many years was lit, leading to Isaac Newton to intervene to explain that the Great Pyramid had been built using two types of feet: a "vulgar" one and a "sacred" one. We know that these descriptions were respected by all the other researchers.

178

We can already see that each of these scientists used logic: starting with real elements, all of them verified, they could make deductions or discoveries that responded to what one could expect from a human mind, even a most brilliant one, something that happened in the earliest time of what history calls the Modern Age.

If we start with the unprecedented

Egyptologists have written that the first dynasty of the pharaohs began between the years 3,000 and 2,778 BC. However, in his work "The Mysteries of the Great Pyramids" André Pochan claimed that Manethon moved the birth of Egypt to the year 30,544 BC, that is, when human beings must have been living in caves and had barely begun to use fire. If in addition we discover from the same historian that the Dynasty of the Gods began in this remote period, we must believe that creatures that had been walking erect on their two legs, who communicated using guttural sounds, were only hunters and were obsessed with the need to survive could not be called thus, since their average age cannot have even reached twenty.

These gods must have been extra-terrestrials who taught a highly select group of Egyptians how to cultivate the land, fish the Nile, speak, build their dwellings far from the mountain slopes and write. In brief, they transformed them into a true civilisation.

But Manethon's chronology provides many elements of millennial Egypt: it tells us that the Dynasty of the Gods lived for 13,900 years, was then followed by a Dynasty of the Semi-Gods, who maintained their power through 1,255 years. These were then followed by a Dynasty of the Kings, whose period of dominance covered 2,367 years. There was also an almost 60-century long stage in which Egypt was at the mercy of the Spirits of Death. Finally, the pharaohs and everything we know about appeared.

Do we dare speculate with dates so beyond archaeological proof?

There is a remote possibility that the extremely long periods corresponding to the Dynasties of the Gods, Semi-gods and Kings coincided with paradise, but not with that mentioned in the Bible. Humanity learned to live in harmony, contented with everything it learned and continuing to evolve toward perfection as its own conquests materialised. It did not know selfishness, envy, pride and everything that could distance it from the others. It lived, enjoyed, procreated and possibly even died in old age, and it was the mirror of a fabulous civilisation that came from outer space.

But something must have happened for the category of Gods to fall to Semi-gods, and then to Kings. This fall obviously took place after millennia of enjoying a paradise where the Nile flooded regularly, the desert wind never blew bothersome sand, and oases were not needed because Egypt itself provided everything needed.

Atlantis may have existed in this period.

After so many years of limitless prosperity, suddenly came the time of the Spirits of the Dead. We should view these as geological cataclysms that divided the continents, made the mountains shoot up toward the heavens to form ranges such as the Himalayas, and what had been a paradise became a hell; magma tells us that it washed away all living beings, perhaps like a first Great Flood, and led to the sinking of Atlantis.

But groups of human beings were able to survive, perhaps as ignorant as the cave dwellers at the mercy of disease, who would take many years to learn how to work the fields, until they were once again visited by an extra-terrestrial: Osiris.

The god Osiris

The theory that Osiris was an extra-terrestrial is shared by various modern Egyptian scholars. Mythology tells us that Osiris was the god of the dead and the underground world (also of fertility), that he was married to his sister Isis and had a son named Horus.

One of the most famous pyramidologists, the Frenchman, Georges Barbarin, wrote the following:

Between the messianic prophecies that spread throughout the Orient, I should highlight one of them, dating from the year 3,000 BC, which said that the Messiah would be born on the first day of the month of Tisri and would die on the 15th day of the month of Nisan. These prophecies did not only mention his dates of birth and death, but they also specified the details of his life, of the ministry and passion of the Messiah, as well as his victory over death and the tomb.

Later, these predictions deviated from their objective by the Egyptian fathers who replaced the Messiah with Osiris. And this explains why some have wrongly seen the worship of Osiris in the tales of the gospel.

The fact that the symbol of Christ and that of the Pyramid are identical is even more obvious if we continue to search in the ancient Egyptian texts.

According to Marsham Adams, the Messiah was in them constantly, called the names 'Master of the Pyramid', 'Master of the Year', 'Master of Death and Resurrection'...

In this case, Barbarin even doubts the fact that Osiris was a Messiah, while many scholars assign him this role after proving that he was an extra-terrestrial.

Von Däniken's fascinating theories

To Erich von Däniken, the ancient Egyptians were helped by 'unknown intelligent beings'. Between 10,000 and 40,000 years ago, powerfully intelligent extra-terrestrials landed somewhere on our planet and did not hesitate to unite carnally with creatures they came across. In this way 'homo sapiens' were born. Shortly thereafter, the 'men from outer space' left, certain that they had sowed the simian with great knowledge, and they successively returned to help the evolution and progress of the human race: they taught the basics of metallurgy, agriculture, written language and many other things.

Von Däniken supports his theories by the unquestionable fact that all ancient cultures talk about winged gods and flying machines, which are two primitive expressions that attempt to describe aeronautical devices that they did not understand. However, they must have viewed them very differently than the initiates, who had the immense privilege of establishing contact with the extra-terrestrials, learning from them and progressing. However, they were always careful not to spread their knowledge, as if they were frightened that if they became 'something for the common masses', they might lose all their magical value.

We have a great deal of evidence that in the pyramids, sphinxes and obelisks of Egypt the messages, prophecies and all the wisdom from a fabulous library had to have been interpreted by highly educated people, free of prejudices and ready to learn the truth without letting fear overcome them. This is one of Von Däniken's messages.

When did the inventions reach the people?

In Egypt, iron was preferably used in the religious ceremonies called 'the mouth'. Given its composition, it should be considered 'meteoric iron', since the word that defined it was associated with the sky (in some ways it is an ancient synonym for the modern word 'metallurgy'). This indicated the sacred nature of the material, which prevented it from being used for vulgar purposes. It was denied to the people, so that archaeologists have only been able to locate small instruments made with this metal inside the temples and the pyramids.

This mystery could be associated with the studied carried out by Mircea Eliade on the sacred, mysterious nature of the Egyptian guild of ironmongers. It was forbidden under penalty of death to divulge the secret of iron smelting. This mystery ended up being discovered by some crusaders, perhaps after paying gold to Arabs. Thus it reached Europe.

The wheel was also known for millennia only by the high priests and pharaohs; however, it could not be used beyond the thresholds of the temples and palaces. We do not know the name of the monarch who decided to use it on war chariots, as if it were a foreign invention bought to strengthen their armies. Perhaps it was to confront an enemy that already used vehicles on wheels and not dragged by rollers led to this charade being devised. In spite of the fact carriages had been placed before the altars of the gods filled with ointments, perfumes, diadems and other ceremonials elements for many centuries.

The obvious conclusion leads us to assume that the ancient Egyptians, the initiates, used iron and the wheel, as well as a great number of inventions. But they kept them in the secrecy of their temples, which in the long term would lead to serious, archaeological problems. Logically, the lack of evidence in many of the disinterments and excavations led people to believe that this technology did not exist.

However, the transport of the great granite blocks from the Nile quarries, or from there to the esplanades where the pyramids were being built, lead one to believe that they must have used more effective means than rollers, sliding paths and simple human pulling. Also, when seeing the cleanness of the cuts in the quarries, of which there is evidence, along with the perfection of the edges of the granite blocks, we are obliged to imagine that they are not the work of highly sharpened stones. Nevertheless, since no one has found an element that cuts iron, traditional science assumes that it does not exist.

But, are we not using our imaginations in this chapter?

The quarries, the surgeons, the high priests, the soldiers, the embalmers and many other highly-ranked professionals knew about iron, but not just anyone. The technology of its smelting must have been so perfect, perhaps superior to what we have today, that it allowed them to open the cranium of an ill person in a second or cut the hardest granite without ruining its edges... Have we not considered the possibility that lasers were used?

We shall not be the ones to discard this super-modern tool, which might have reached the hands of Egyptian specialists after having been trained by extra-terrestrials.

The behaviour of cosmic rays

The astrophysicist Luis W. Ivarez, who was awarded the Nobel Prize for Physics in 1968, decided to investigate

Khafre's pyramid using cosmic rays. He was convinced that by using this resource he could discover if there were more secret chambers and passageways. Doctor Ivarez himself expressed it this basically:

Any student of physics knows that cosmic radiation deteriorates when it crosses the atmosphere. Eighty percent of this energy reaches the Earth in the form of mesons of a medium magnitude, or highly penetrating mions which can quite easily penetrate any rock. I understood that if we placed mion counters in the lower part of the pyramid, we could find out if they had crossed an empty space, since they travel more quickly through air than through hard rock.

In the spring of 1967, a piece of equipment weighing thirty tonnes was taken to the Giza area. Its installation took more than three months, but when the experiment was about to begin it had to be interrupted because the Six-Day War between Israel and Egypt broke out.

One year later, Professor Ivarez and his team were able to complete the investigation with highly disconcerting results. Let us once again allow Professor Ivarez explain it:

From the first instant we could not hide our surprise. The presence of ions in the Royal Chamber was much greater than we had imagined despite the fact that we made them with an angle of three degrees. In general, we were measuring 84 mions per minute, using a cone located at the top of the pyramid which we had placed at an angle of 70 degrees. As the days went by, we noticed that the measurements changed, until the computers revealed the existence of an empty area in the middle... We had done it!

But, while we were all shaking hands, one of the engineers told us that the computer screen had changed. The shadow no longer appeared. Highly disappointed, we made several further checks, with such irregular results that we reached the conclusion that a mysterious force was taking pains to interrupt all of our investigations...

Since many millions of dollars had been invested in the research, it had to continue by changing locations successively throughout many months. Finally, Professor Ivarez had to admit failure to the journalists:

Perhaps the geometry of the pyramid suffers an error that we have not been able to discover, which would allow us to give a logical response to the uselessness of all our efforts... But I am more inclined to believe that it is something else. I do not mind calling it magic, the curse of the pharaohs or whatever you might imagine. The truth is that an energy that is capable of challenging all the laws of science is acting inside the pyramid...

When these results are examined, the results obtained with the replicas of the Great Pyramid come to mind. Is it possible that this power emanating from it, capable of preserving food inside it and exercising a good number of positive influences, is due to cosmic energy?

The coincidences in the pyramids

In all the places in the world where pyramids were built, whether in Central America, Egypt or South America, there exist legends that talk about tall, white, blond-haired, blue-eyed beings. The Pre-Columbian indigenous people in Peru called them the "big ears". It is written that one of the things that most surprised the Spaniards when they reached the Caribbean and then Mexico and other places on the American continent was the fact that they were received 'as if they had been expecting us'.

In the Yucatan peninsula, the natives gathered to greet the Spanish ships with songs and flowers because they considered the men gods. Many theories attempt to explain these deeds.

First there is the one that tells us that thousands of years ago Alaska and Siberia were joined, which allowed for the great migrations of Asians toward what would be called the American continent. At that time, a group of those immigrants must have known the techniques for building pyramids, while having also learnt the basis of a highly advanced astronomy, an idea that is not shared by the archaeologists who have followed these migratory cycles, whose origins correspond to human beings who only knew about fire and hunting.

Once Alaska and Siberia separated, forming a barrier that was not passable by the means of navigation at the time, the inhabitants of the future America had not yet reached Mexico. We should take into account that they moved following their prey or after being kicked off their lands by other peoples. This leads us to believe that their knowledge reached them 'from outer space', through extra-terrestrials or the inhabitants of Atlantis.

There are theories that place the submerged Atlantis in the famous Bermuda Triangle. A second possibility, which would explain the cordial treatment the Spaniards received, comes from the arrival of Templar navigators in around the thirteenth century. But this is a question we shall not even begin to pursue.

In conclusion: nothing definitive

All the scientists who have carried out research on the pyramids recognise the extraordinary technology used by their architects. They handled highly evolved techniques which easily surpass those in the twentieth century. For example, their drills could penetrate up to one hundred times more powerfully than the drills used in the most modern petroleum industry.

When we look at the marble covering of the primitive pyramids, the majority of Egyptologists recognises that they were worked according to the most rigorous rules of the optical industry of today. To provide an exact idea of the magnitude of this work, we believe it is enough to say that the drilling of all these marble pieces, sixteen tonnes each, represents a feat comparable with the lens of the famous telescope at the Palomar Observatory. But we know that this covering was composed of 25,000 blocks, which means that the Egyptian artists from the fourth dynasty managed to 'manufacture in series' that which modern industry is only capable of making one by one.

When we bear in mind the error in measuring the base of the Great Pyramid, which is barely 0.11 inches, we are forced to wonder what means the Egyptian architects used when we can only do this using the so-called 'Invar tapes' (an alloy with a low coefficient of thermal dilation) and using precision thermometers that monitor the temperature.

As a final example, we can use the parallel existing between the pyramids of Cheops and Khafre, whose faces and bases are absolutely parallel; geometricians in 1995, and even those in 2000, will never accomplish something similar.

Given all this information we can ask this question: "can traditional history really continue to say that ancient Egypt had nothing more than rural technology?" We must either laugh or cry, because it could be said that there are great powers in the world that refuse to accept the obvious, especially when 'that which breaks all the established norms' comes into play. However, many of us believe that there exists more than what our eyes can see, that we have a brain that no one can limit, and that our curiosity is so infinite that after trembling before the unknown, we continue forward because 'it is better to know than to be kept in the dark.

BIBLIOGRAPHY

Álvarez López, José: *El enigma de las Pirámides.*
Asimov, Isaac: *The Egyptians.*
Atienza, Juan G.: *Los supervivientes de la Atlántida.*
Barbarin, Georges: *Le secret de la Grande Pyramide.*
Bergier, J. and Pauwels, J.: *La rebelión de los brujos.*
Berman, Franz: *El enigma de las Pirámides.*
Champdor, Albert: *Le livre des morts des anciens égyptiens.*
Däniken, Erich von: *Profeta del pasado.*
García Gallo, Luis: *De las mentiras de la Egiptología a las verdades de la Gran Pirámide.*
Grilletto, Renato: *Il mistero delle mummie.*
Guirao, P.: *El enigma de las pirámides de Egipto.*
Guirao, P.: *El enigma de la Esfinge y las pirámides de Gizeh.*
Hasch, Annie: *El poder de las pirámides.*
Herodotus: *Book II.*
Hodges, Peter: *How the Pyramids were Built.*
L. de Gérin, Ricard: *Histoire de l'Occultisme.*
Lange, Kurt: *Pyramiden, Sphinxe, Pharaonen.*
Montet, Pierre: *Vie quotidienne en Égypte au temps des Ramsès.*
Osman, Ahmed: *Strangers in the Valley of the Kings.*
Salas, Emilio and Cano, Ramón: *O poder das pirâmides, 2.*
Thompkins, Peter: *Secrets of the Great Pyramid.*
Toth, Max: *Pyramid Prophecies.*

189

Toth, Max and Nielsen, Greg: *Pyramid Power.*
Vanderberg, Philipp: *The Curse of the Pharaoh.*
Walker, Martin: *La maldición de los faraones.*
El gran libro de las Profecías (Martínez Roca).
Egipto, tras las huellas de los faraones (Aguilar Universal).
Egipto – Mitos y Leyendas (M. E. Editores).

INDEX